Journey to Health

Living Well from the Inside Out

www.TheWisdomBuffet.com

Copyright Notice

Dedication

We dedicate this book to Angi Ma Wong, a colleague, friend, and fellow *Wisdom Buffet Writer.* Angi suffered with breast cancer for twenty-six years. Her tenacity and courage is a testament to how she lived with this disease, giving it the perspective and respect it deserved. It was a privilege to work with Angi, and her voice will live on between the pages of this book.

We also dedicate this book to those in search of a sound mind, body, and spirit. We hope this book will bring you closer to that wonderful gift.

> *- The Wisdom Buffet Writers*

Preface

It is said that without health, we have nothing. We know this to be true when we become ill or incapacitated. Like the old saying, *"you don't know what you've got till it's gone,"* can apply to all things in life, but especially when it comes to our health.

Health used to be defined as "the state of being free from illness or injury." It was later re-defined as "a state of complete physical, mental and social well-being" and not merely the absence of disease or infirmity. So, what is good health, really?

In the second of an eight book series, *The Wisdom Buffet Writers* bring to you their latest book: *Journey to Health; Living Well from the Inside Out.* These eight contributing authors, all with the commonality of being Feng Shui Consultants, share with you their perception of what health means to them and how we might capture it for ourselves.

We invite you to explore a collection of short stories, how-to-guidelines, and wisdom handed down from the masters; written in an easy-to-read format that can help you get started and keep you on the path to good health and well-being from the inside out.

Table of Contents

When Cancer Surprises You, You Can Surprise It Back

By Janet Mitsui Brown

I remember the month and year very well. In early November I was in my 30s, feeling invincible, with no plans for the future. I was watching the actress Ann Jillian on television urging her viewers to do a self-breast exam. Idly, I felt my right breast, and oddly enough there was a small lump. Hmmmm. I had a mammogram a few weeks later and it was negative. The doctor said there was no need for further action, but for some reason I heard myself feel the need for certainty, so I declared I wanted a biopsy. The doctor was reluctant but the medical coverage was available, so he agreed to schedule one for me.

They found the malignancy in my right breast three weeks later, and four days before Christmas I had my first breast mastectomy.

I was lucky because we found the cancer early. And that is the key -- early detection is of primary importance to living without cancer.

Nine years and many mammograms later, cancer was detected in my left breast duct cell. However this time I couldn't feel it. It was an in-situ cancer -- a pre-invasive breast cancer -- and it was discovered before it broke through the wall of the duct, before it could grow into the tissue of the breast -- to flow into my lymph nodes and, subsequently, into the rest of my body. And fourteen years after that, I found an innocent small lump on my lower leg (of all places), and my dermatologist found this to be cancerous as well. Removal was easy and quick.

The fortunate lesson was early detection. But what does this really mean? It means that I was lucky to get three warnings before real damage occurred.

And so, almost thirty years later, my mantra for today is:

- Listen to my body
- Bolster my immune system
- Work on positive body qi flow

Listening to My Body

There are seven important energy points in the body, and in the tantric tradition they are referred to as Chakras. I like to refer to them as seven major body vortexes. The Hindu and Buddhist tantric traditions believe the seven chakras reveal different energies in vision and body. And Qi Gong uses the chakras to examine the energy flow in the body. The functions of my chakras are to keep my body -- mentally, physically and spiritually, in balance. If something is not right, my intuition works with me, and so everyday I listen to each of the seven chakras as

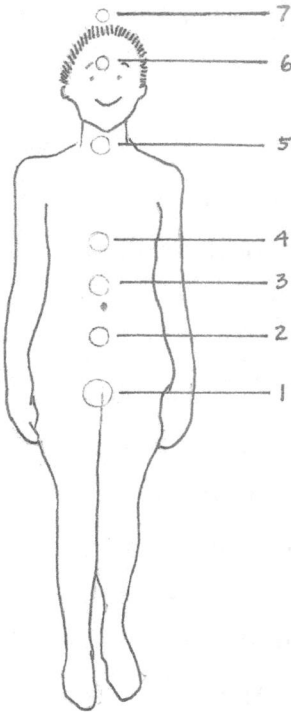

indicated below in Diagram A:

Each morning when it is quiet, I visualize the first chakra: the base chakra, the area at the front and back tailbone area.

I then visualize the second, the sacral chakra: the Chinese referenced dan tien two fingers below the belly button.

The third chakra: the solar plexus located above the belly button in the upper abdomen. The fourth chakra: the heart chakra in the area where the heart is located. The fifth chakra is located at my throat. The sixth chakra is my third eye, between my two eyes, so important for intuition. And finally, the seventh chakra is the crown chakra, located at the top of my head. It only takes a few minutes, but it's surprising what I hear, what I feel, and what I learn, about my body. If I have a stomachache, I can feel it in the second chakra. Perhaps I am scared, I can feel my heart pumping (4th chakra) and throat tighten (5th chakra). If I'm worried, it might affect my head (6th and 7th chakra). I can identify if I am in balance or not, and I can start to pinpoint an energy that needs to be examined and perhaps modified.

Bolstering My Immune System

One of my doctors once told me that everyone has pre-cancer cells in the body. But what makes them grow is a conundrum of factors. A strengthened immune system can help protect my body, leading the charge against abnormal substances that lead to a malignancy -- not all the time, but significantly most of the time. We hear what bolsters the immune system time and again, but it's worth repeating:

<u>Eat more fruits and vegetables</u> and less animal protein and fat.

<u>Exercise</u>: I am an advocate of tai chi gong, yoga and walking, but do whatever is comfortable and convenient to you. Just do it!

<u>Reduce stress</u>. I said reduce, not eliminate! Stress comes with living socially in our environment but meditation, exercise, and listening to my body tells me how to live with stress. I can choose stress, reduce stress, or walk away from it.

<u>Sleep</u>. I am not a sleeper, but a good shower or steam and relaxation choices before bed, help me sleep soundly. What a marvelous feeling it is in the morning when I have slept well.

<u>Don't smoke, drink smart and in moderation</u>, try to use prescription

drugs and aspirin in moderation when appropriate.

Educate yourself in finding herbs that enhance your immune system.

And finally, take vitamins to supplement your food intake

Work on Positive Qi Flow in the Body

A positive healing influence in my life is working with the Shaolin Wushu Center in Los Angeles. I started doing tai chi in Palisades Park overlooking the Santa Monica ocean with my "sifu" ("teacher") Zong Jianmei, and instantly fell in love with the exercise. It's movement in the park with an ocean breeze; it's wind and water, feng shui meditation at its best.

Before we do the tai chi movement we circulate the qi in our bodies by doing a series of internal qi gong exercises, practicing balanced bodily cultivation.

It is the beginning of a meditative practice, concentrating on pressure points related to the body. I believe this is essential exercise to bolster my immune system, circulating the energy in my body as often as I can.

Let's begin by applying pressure points on the head, because that is the first thing we see in the morning, and the easiest way to begin. Applying gentle pressure to different parts of the face and head circulates the qi – the life flow – in different parts of the body, according to Chinese tradition. It's easy and practical, and can be done anytime of the day, but how easy is it to do in the morning when I've just risen, and I'm looking in the mirror.

The Qi Gong Series Begins with the Head

You can do this simple exercise inside the home -- by looking in a mirror. Or you can do it outdoors -- without a mirror

-- enjoying the sounds and feel of nature simultaneously. Wherever you are, stand balanced with feet slightly apart.

I take the index and middle fingers of both hands to begin – holding them together, with each thumb holding its respective ring and pinky fingers.

Use Diagram B to follow along with me.

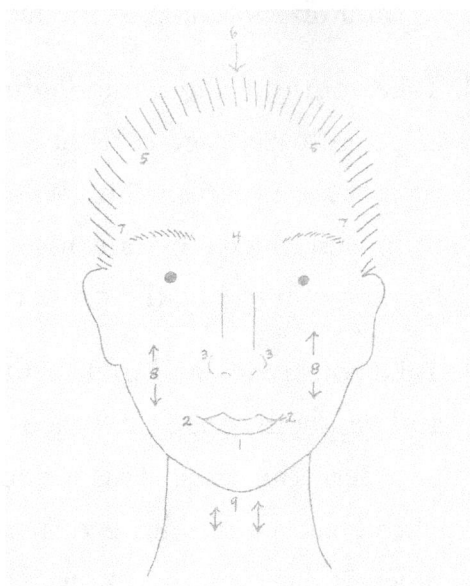

Diagram B

1. Take your index and middle fingers, and gently massage the area right below your lips. This balances your appetite and helps you eat appropriately and maintain a good diet.

2. Take your index and middle fingers and gently massage both sides of the corners of your lips. This helps to minimize swelling in the face.

3. Take your index and middle fingers, and gently massage each side of your lower nostrils. This will help to loosen mucus in your nose, helping you to breathe properly.

4. Take your index and middle fingers and gently massage the space between your eyes. This is your sixth chakra and third eye. This will relieve tired eyes and minimize an aching head.

5. Take your index and middle fingers and gently massage each side just above the outer eyebrow, at your hairline, to minimize dizziness or an aching head.

6. Take your index and middle fingers and gently massage the very center of your head at your hairline, to work on an aching head or brain issues.

7. Take your index and middle fingers and gently massage each side of your temples, at the hairline, in line with your eyebrows, for headaches.

8. Take your index, middle, ring and pinky fingers and place them on your cheeks and move your skin gently up and down to help you with teeth issues so you can nourish yourself properly.

9. Take your index, middle and ring

fingers and gently massage down
and up on your neck to balance
breathing, swallowing, and the throat.

It is difficult to generalize about cancer threats. Each case is personal. Genetic predisposition has a dramatic effect on each person's risk factors. Environmental dispositions can have a powerful influence. As a survivor, I do believe, however, we can increase our odds for survival with early detection, by either the medical profession or most significantly, our own personal sense of our body.

We live in a fast paced world, with many opportunities and resources to live a good life. However, we need to remember to slow down, smell the roses, check our chakras, take care of ourselves, and make sure our energy is circulating positively to continue to live in joy.

Here they are; the three mantras I've

learned to rely on, to live a better life, to protect myself as best I can from serious illness, and enjoy each day:

- Listen to my body
- Bolster my immune system
- Work on positive body qi flow

And if, or when, cancer surprises you, you can surprise it back. I've been there; I'm a cancer survivor.

Living a Healthy Life on the Go

By Belinda Mendoza

I have always led a fast-paced life. In my corporate job I traveled extensively and ate out most of the time. It was always a challenge to keep my immune system strong and weight down.

I moved to a city where I now live and the pollen count often gets off the charts high. It often gets the better of me and is funny that I am writing this chapter on Health while nursing a head and chest cold I've had for a week now. It brings on new symptoms each day for me to examine. Its times like this I really do appreciate the overall good health I have enjoyed for many years. It has not always been this way. For many years I endured horrible, debilitating migraine headaches. If you have not had migraines it is hard to explain to others the pain you feel . It never goes away and you feel nauseous and achy all over. Sometimes I could not see to take exams in college and would run to the bathroom to throw up. I had them for over twenty years. My mom had them for over forty.

I can't remember a day growing up when she didn't have one. I was told that when I was around two years old I would mimic my mom by walking around the house placing my little hand on my head while saying, "heck ache, heck ache", or something like that.

Mom always had many super-sized aspirin bottles on hand and a product called Malox to calm her stomach. Tylenol did not come around until later on. She was so used to regular aspirin she felt the Tylenol did not work as fast. Later years, she developed bleeding ulcers, finally passing out at work. The doctor told her it was

from years of taking so much aspirin. It
wore out her stomach lining.

She worked full-time while I was growing
up, then came home to make us dinner,
do laundry, get us ready for bed, then start
over. It was exhausting to watch even as a
child. She was a young woman at the time
in her twenties. This time in her life had to
be so stressful for her. My father worked
but was never around except for evenings
and weekends and did most of the outside
work on our house when he was home.

My mother learned her cooking skills
from her mother, my grandmother. My
grandmother had 14 children! My mom
was one the youngest of those kids. My
grandfather who was in the military was
also never home when she grew up.

Grandma, as we called her, raised all the
kids by herself doing the cooking and
cleaning while working several jobs. She

died in her 80's from artery disease and the last ten years of her life were spent at home in bed. I am sure she was just plain exhausted. Her poor body just couldn't take anymore.

We always loved going to my grandma's for holidays because she was such a good cook. Everything she made tasted great to us. She made delicious assorted cakes, cookies with icing, cupcakes with sprinkles, and all the stuff kids like. I don't ever remember a time going to visit where there wasn't a table of assorted treats to choose from. She was also great with large Mexican dinners of homemade tamales, chicken mole, rice, beans, and more. See, we are from a Hispanic family and eating is the main thing we do when we get together. It's all about the food and drink. It is how we socialize, ease tension within the family, and just plain get along.

Here is where the problem was though….

one of the things that made all the dishes taste so good was that they were either fried or made with lard or cooking oil. Homemade flour tortillas made with lard were a staple item. We spent our summers with our other Mexican grandmother who made them fresh for us each day. So, growing up in my family where my mother cooked all our meals, we all ate food that was tasty but heavily fried.

I don't remember eating much Mexican food at our house but mom made all the comfort foods like fried chicken, meat loaf, fried fish, fried eggs, bacon. Rarely, did we eat fresh vegetables. If we had veggies, they were coated with butter, bacon grease, or gravy. Salads were rare. If we ate broccoli it had lots of cheese on it. Most Hispanic meal plates were all brown…rice, beans, with some whites like potatoes, noodles, tortillas with meat combinations.

My mom grew up being so responsible

so young that it was and still is hard for her to delegate. She never taught me how to cook. I remember taking a home economics class and our homework was to make a dish at home. Our parents could help but we had to do it ourselves. My mom wouldn't let me do it. She said I would just make a mess in the kitchen and she didn't have the extra time to clean it up. She assumed I could not do it. Looking back I think she just had too much on her plate and it was one more thing to deal with.

Now, just about all of us in my immediate family, have high cholesterol. Were we either born with it or was it a result of my mother's cooking? I think it was both. We never had a chance as kids to correct it. I remember being really thin in college weighing about 105 lbs. at 5'3" and my cholesterol was over 300. Now that I am in my 50's and heavier it is lower but not where it needs to be for good long term health.

It has been a challenge for me as an adult to eat right. I know all the things to do but I keep going back to the comfort foods I grew up with and the easiest ways to get food.

Today, I am single and an entrepreneur so I eat out a lot of the time for social, networking, or business reasons. This has not only helped me pack on the pounds but is also highly addictive. Most of the foods in restaurants have substances that increase appetite and make you gain weight. Yes, I would love to have a personal chef like Oprah, where I could come home and have healthy and tasty meals ready for me, but that is not in my future(at least not now)...I want to think positively as it could happen! But... I am not giving up.

I continue to exercise even if it's to walk my dogs. I buy healthy food to keep in the fridge so if I feel the need to snack it has some nutritional value. When I eat out I choose healthier options as much as possible. When I shop at the grocery store I buy fewer things with sugar in them. Sugar was and is the main diet challenge in Hispanic families. It is why many are so overweight and that diabetes and colon cancer are their main killers. Too much sugar and not enough roughage with fruits or vegetables.

I have a tenant who rents a room from me in my home. He says he never has had vegetables and doesn't eat them at all. He's a male Hispanic in his early 40's. I got him drinking V8 juice. It's a start.

Alcoholism ranks up there with the bad in their diet too but isn't it sugar anyway? I keep my alcohol consumption to a glass of red wine once in awhile, like a couple of times a week if at all. I never have smoked.

While I can blame my cultural heritage
for my less than optimum health, I know
it doesn't help anything. It just makes
me understand why I have the cravings,
desires for certain foods, and lack of desire
to cook. I know now that I can eat these
foods in a healthier way. I can add salad to
my rice and bean plate. Eat corn tortillas
instead of flour. Since I live alone, I can
choose any food to fix or eat. It is a luxury
that many do not have who has to prepare
food for others in the home. I am grateful
for this freedom and want to use it wisely.

So, if you are in this category of cultural
eating, don't feel alone. We can make a
difference and break the chain of any poor
eating habits. One thing our grandparents
had in their favor is that they did not eat
processed food like we do today. It just was
not available nor could they afford it. Mine
ate rice, beans, corn or flour tortillas. Some

meat was added when there was extra money.

Whatever your culture, it has some good and some bad things about its diet. Choose the good things. Don't try to change it completely and keep things simple. I still eat rice and beans but in moderation.

Here are some Easy and Fun Ways I Have Learned to Keep Myself Healthy :

- **Eat only foods you love.** Make eating a pleasurable experience. You will eat less because you have not deprived yourself. If some foods are not good for you, like sugar, eat in moderation or find some healthier option.

- **Make sure everything tastes good.** Season to taste. Don't try to go cold turkey and not eat things the way you like. This is the fastest way to binge or overeat on the bad foods.

- **Avoid processed foods** as much as possible. Pretty much anything wrapped in cellophane is not good for you. They have low nutritional content and lots of calories.

- **Add more greens** /veggies to whatever you eat. This will give your meal the balance it needs with the roughage to clean out your colon and keep it working well. If eating a hamburger, add plenty of sprouts and lettuce to it. I knew a small vegetarian Indian man who would go to McDonald's and order a salad with fries, when he was in between appointments. He knew it was not his healthiest option but it was quick and he made sure he had the salad.

- **Drink lots of water.** I drink water with lemon daily to cleanse my colon. Water also fills me up.

- **Make simple dishes** (things that only take about ten minutes prep time) to start. Once you get in this habit you will be motivated to try other recipes. Don't try to be a gourmet cook unless that is your passion. You'll just get frustrated. Baked salmon with a salad and some fruit for dessert works fine. Sometimes I even put a glaze or a sauce on my salmon. I do have a sweet tooth so if you are not a diabetic it's an option.

- **Prepare meals ahead of time**. Use Sunday afternoons to chop veggies, prepare and store foods you can heat or cook during the week. When you are driving home and you know that good tasty food awaits you only taking a few minutes to fix will ease the temptation to order out like I often do.

- **Set up your refrigerator** for health success. In the art of feng shui which I practice, your kitchen represents your health. It is important that it is free of clutter and organized for easy use. One thing people often forget is how important the refrigerator is. You open it many times in a day. When you open it, you should see fresh things. Display your food so it looks inviting. A glass bowl filled with various colored vegetables, a pretty pitcher of water with lemons, a bowl of fresh fruit, all make you feel energized and healthy when you look at it. Dispose of anything expired, not being used, or old. Only keep fresh items. This will help you stay on your path to wellness and longevity.

- **Carry healthy snacks** in your purse or car. If you are starving when driving home you will get tempted to drive through a fast food window even if you have fresh and tasty food at home. Carry a mixture of nuts like walnuts and almonds. Have some easy to eat fruit that will not spoil right away like easy to peel tangelos or small apples. Make sure your stash is always fresh and do vary it so you don't get bored. In our blistery hot summers there is no way to keep anything in the car so I carry a small cooler with snacks and plenty of water. At the very l least, the snacks moderate my blood sugar so I can make a healthy decision on what to eat later.

- **Eat Protein late at night**. If you are a late-nighter like I often am,

you will get hungry by 11:00pm,
especially if you ate dinner at 6pm.
A holistic physician gave me this tip
that I find really works well. Eat a
small piece of protein like a piece
of chicken or turkey. This will not
only moderate your blood sugar but
take away the hunger pangs. Eating
cereal, toast, or some other sugary
snack just has calories and can
elevate your blood sugar levels while
not even satisfying your hunger. I
knew a guy who ate four bowls
of cereal each night for about four
months. When I saw him I didn't
recognize him. He had gained so
much weight and was previously
trim. He admitted he needed to
stop the late night cereal eating.
I really like physician Dr. Mehmet
Oz who has a national health show
on television for his knowledgeable

and sensible advice He says it is not the late night eating that puts on weight, it is the number of calories you take in all day long. I was glad to hear that but by the time 11pm hits, most of us have had more than our calories in a day. I know I have so I limit what I eat after about 7pm.

- **Meditate**. Do whatever you can to reduce stress. Stress can cause overeating and weight gain. I meditate each day even if for a few minutes. I take time to breathe in and breathe out. Sing, journal, or listen to calming music. Just take time to do nothing. Listen to calming music on your way home in traffic to lessen the anxiety that can cause binge eating.

- **Do whatever form of exercise makes you happy**. I am not and will never be an athlete. I always wanted to be and maybe in my younger days had my parents put me in some athletic program I might have excelled. I was really good at softball and volleyball. I do like to exercise but just can't keep up anything consistently that I don't love. Some days I do yoga, some I walk, swim, or bicycle. I love to dance and do that whenever I can even if in my living room. Just move. You will feel better.

- **Get support**. Join a group of other's who want to be fit. It can even be a few friends who just want to walk each day in your neighborhood.

- **Use alternative methods**. I learned the healing art of Reiki to rid myself of those debilitating migraines. You can go to: www. reiki.org to find out more about it. Once I learned this gentle art, my headaches went away. No other medication helped. It is good for stress reduction, weight management, and energy as well. So today I knock on wood to say that other than an occasional head or allergy cold, I have not been to a doctor in over ten years. I do not take prescription drugs of any sort. I am a believer in combining eastern with western medicine. Sometimes you just need an antibiotic to get you through something. I do get regular acupuncture, chiropractic, massages, and energy work to keep my energy levels up and prevent illness. I believe in using it all. Whatever you know and have access to-use it. I take supplements to

boost my immune system. I am still
working to lower my cholesterol
and lose extra pounds but all in all I
have good continuous energy.
I don't think you have to be extreme
to be fit. It won't last anyway. It's
not good feng shui. Feng Shui is all
about harmony. If I have learned
anything from being a practitioner,
its that going with the flow of life
is much easier. Do what feels best
to you first, the rest will come. If
it's just adding some veggies twice a
week to your diet, it's a good start.
I bought a vegetable juicer and
started juicing. This way I am sure
to get my veggies.

- **Eat mindfully** so you can savor
  each bite and enjoy the process of
  eating. You will not only eat less
  but feel better afterwards. If I can

sit down with just my food and no outside disturbances I can imagine it nourishing my body.

- **Be grateful** for the abundance of food you have access to and consume. This gives the feeling that there will always be food so you don't have to eat more than your body needs. Appreciating what I am eating puts me in the present moment and aware of its importance. I like showing gratitude for all who brought the food to the table like any animals who were sacrificed, any workers in the fields, those in factories who packaged the food, etc. Whatever your cultural background or heritage or habits, you can create new ones. Just make sure it works for you and that you are happy with it. I find it must fit my body and lifestyle. If going to your parents' home for Sunday dinners is sabotaging your health plan, spend less time there. See them once a month instead of once a week. Join the YMCA like I have done and spend time there instead.

Remember there are many solutions to being fit. Find the one that is right for YOU! It is an investment in your future.

I love this quote by Mahatma Ghandi:

"Your Health is your Real Wealth".

We can have both! Wishing you great health today and tomorrow..

Health Lessons from Elizabeth Taylor

By Katherine Graham

There's a joke about Elizabeth Taylor that goes something like this: Late in her career, during the time she was married to Senator John Warner (marriage number seven, husband number six), Elizabeth appeared at a press stop in a small town in England. Several stout, middle-aged British ladies in their boxy house dresses and sensible shoes lined up amongst the throng of gawkers and paparazzi. One of the ladies, getting a glimpse of Elizabeth Taylor not in her tiny-waisted, big-bosomed heyday but in the fleshy form she had succumbed to, stated, "We always wanted to look like Elizabeth Taylor. Now we do!"

Child star turned international beauty and superstar, long-term abuse of alcohol, drugs and destructive relationships with both men and food, left the once utterly gorgeous, world-famous, exceedingly wealthy Elizabeth Taylor struggling to find balance, peace and contentment in what, by all respects, should have been a charmed life. Her lifestyle of glorious excess may have looked glamorous and appealing from the outside but these choices led to major health issues, numerous surgeries and a very public battle with her weight.

What can we learn about our own health from Elizabeth Taylor? Quite a lot. Both from her slimmed-down and shimmering glory days and in her later, more secluded wheelchair-bound years with her dog, Daisy, by her side. Elizabeth Taylor was a lot of things but she wasn't one to suffer from illusions. In honor of her straightforward, adventurous manner, I'll give it to you straight:

1. Let food be thy medicine and let thy medicine be food. (And oh, chew slowly.)

Through her own admission to friends and in her 1988 diet book entitled, "Elizabeth Takes Off," Elizabeth Taylor's illustrious indulgences are well documented. At times contradictory, yet always entertaining, her book is a veritable manifesto of the outmoded dietary mores of her day including low-fat dieting. In it, she suggested eating dry toast for breakfast; veggie dips of yogurt, Roquefort cheese and spices; swordfish with lime; steak and peanut butter sandwiches; and a combination of sour cream and cottage cheese poured over fruit. Her self-indulgent side showing through, she allowed readers one "pig out day" each week. When asked what she ate on those days, she replied, "Fried chicken, mashed potatoes with lots of gravy, lima beans, corn, chocolate cake of some kind. But then the next two days you really have to watch it."

Elizabeth hoped her weight loss book would help people yet cholesterol levels soared, waist bands expanded, thunder thighs amassed and the number of casualties from inflammation-based killers like heart disease, cancer and diabetes, increased in record numbers. All despite the manic cardio, calisthenics and the likes of Suzanne Somers showing us how to suggestively squeeze a contraption between our thighs while eating our low-fat T.V. dinners. The rich and famous dieted right alongside the poor and plebeian on high-carb rice cakes, sugar-free yogurt and processed "diet" foods. A trend we now know to be directly linked to the explosion of overweight and obese generations of Americans. The no-fat/low-fat/"bad" fat myth all began with one Dr. Keys' "Seven Countries Study" which officially started in the late 1950s. It was the first large scale epidemiological study of its kind to examine heart risk based on lifestyle and dietary habits. Dr. Keys found that in the countries where people ate more fat, especially saturated fat, there was a higher incidence of heart disease. He, therefore, concluded that fat caused the disease. However, we now know that the problem with this, and similar dietary studies that attempt to pinpoint one specific factor- correlation does not equal causation.

Not only does fat not make you fat, but type trumps percentage. Thanks to the depth of research fueled by the obesity epidemic in America, we know that health and vitality have much more to do with the *quality* of calories and foods we choose rather than simply lack of them.

No longer can we look at the formula for health and weight stability the way we used to, i.e. a calorie is a calorie is a calorie. The way your body utilizes the calories from broccoli vs. cheesecake comes down to a highly complex interaction involving metabolism, intestinal health, genetics, hormones, stress levels, sleep and other bodily systems. It's not just calories in (regardless of the source) vs. calories out (in the amount of fuel burned). What happens when you eat an equal number of calories from a McDonald's cheeseburger as opposed to those from kale and spinach does not lead to identical end results as we first believed. One leads to disease; the other to health.

Fat, fed-up and looking for something to blame, from this extreme we rode a wild pendulum to the other side of the arc and fell head-over-heels in love with

no-carb, low-carb dieting. The seductive
power of diet trends seems to defy our
collective logic and appeals directly to
our most base, reptilian thinking. When
offered a magic pill, we stepped hand
in hand onto the threshold of a mass
state of communal ignorance. Hungry
for a solution, we turned off our better
judgment and gorged on bacon, burgers
(minus the bun of course) and bratwurst
for dinner. With a new common enemy to
target - anything white or that grew in the
ground - we became constipated, sluggish
and irritable, but at least our waists were
growing trim!

Food, quite simply, is information. What,
how much and when you put food
into your body tells whether you are in
times of plenty or living through salad
days. Food programs cells to repair and
regenerate or introduces toxins that wreak
havoc on hormones and prompts cells to

die off or even become cancerous. Food tells your body what time of year it is and whether it's time to lean up or to kick in fat stores. Foods made naturally available and abundant during certain times of the year, for example, nuts, seeds, squashes, and root vegetables in the fall, inform your body it's almost winter and time to store some fat. Likewise, berries, eggs, and the abundance of fruits and vegetables available naturally to us in the spring and summer months, allow us to remain lean and healthy and provide abundant energy to get work done. In winter months, with lower temperatures and few to no fresh foods, our metabolism slows and our fat stores help get us through.

This illustrates the importance of eating seasonally so that our bodies can maintain their natural rhythm, long in place before we had refrigerators. The ready availability of foods year-round and outside their natural growing season has only been the norm for the human race since the ability to grow, store, ship and refrigerate perishable foods, much less than 100 years. When we grew what we ate and ate only what grew during certain seasons, our bodies were in sync with this natural rhythm and our food promoted our health.

The quality of food also triggers important cellular functions such as mitochondrial renewal, stem cell interaction and other biological processes that we are just beginning to appreciate. Our body is unbelievably complex and cells more "intelligent" than we have given much credence to before now. You simply cannot replace quality food, your body's main fuel, with a supplement or quick fix. You cannot trick your cells into health but you can eat your way to a healthy body by eating what God put onto this earth for us and staying away from what man has processed, genetically modified or preserved with chemicals.

What Hippocrates knew thousands of years ago, that food is the foundation of good health, we are now (re)discovering. We control our health, vitality and even gene expression by what we put into and, just as importantly, what we leave out of, our mouths.

2. Healthy means not biting off more than you can chew

Elizabeth Taylor had an open love affair with food. She most enjoyed being holed up in a posh hotel room with her favorite food and wine only a room service call away. She was known to fly in "buckets" of chili from a Chicago restaurant while filming Cleopatra in Rome and pork sausages from London to her set in Paris. She was tempted by all foods, especially those rich or fried. One ill fated night, rushing to scarf down a fried chicken leg while campaigning for John Warner's Senate race, the chicken bone became lodged in her throat and Elizabeth began choking. She required an emergency tracheotomy to save her life. This little known episode is the reason she wore enormous jewels designed to hit at just the place where the scar was left. The lesson here? Respect food and the method with which it enters your body. Chew S-L-O-W-L-Y.

Chewing, with your mouth as ground zero, initiates the digestive process. In fact, this is the very reason that we have specialized taste buds. Not only do taste buds send information to your brain and release hormones that make you feel good when you eat (so that you will seek food out and chew it often enough to survive) but they

also determine whatever you are eating
to be either fats, proteins, etc. which then
signals your stomach to make the specific
enzymes needed to digest what you are
sending down the tube. If you scarf down
your food, these messages aren't as strong,
or complete, and your stomach must then
double its efforts at digestion when the
food hits it, which is greatly taxing to your
entire system.

Just think how you feel after you eat a
giant steak and baked potato compared
to a light soup and salad. Nap anyone?
Lest you can afford the Hope Diamond
to cover up your tracheotomy scar, sit
down, be mindful about what you are
presenting to your system and don't
scarf down your food.

3. Healthy is feeling safe and having a soft place to land

Elizabeth, and other famous, beautiful

women like her, was a favored target of
the press; her life and deeds (good or
bad) relentlessly exploited as content
for magazines and fodder for salacious
stories. Drugs and alcohol figured
prominently in Elizabeth Taylor's life
despite her several valiant attempts to
get sober in the Betty Ford Center for
alcoholism as well as other food addiction
centers. Not having a soft, safe place to
land and be cared for where she could
detox, heal and renew, upon discharge,
Elizabeth went right back to the same bad
habits as before. Which leads to probably
the greatest lesson we could ever learn
from her: stay away from the Richard
Burtons of the world.

4. You are only as good or as healthy as the people you surround yourself with.

An unhealthy lifestyle is seemingly
contagious. Along with their DNA,

parents pass eating habits and lifestyle preferences on to their children. If you spend the majority of your time with people who are overweight or make other unhealthy lifestyle decisions (do drugs, have promiscuous sex, drink excessively), studies show you are more than twice as likely to do the same. Influences are powerful, especially the influence of the people we date, marry or have close relationships with.

Imagine for a moment how different Elizabeth Taylor's life could have been if she had never married Richard Burton. Under his influence, she drank as heavily as he did, took pills, spent and ate extravagantly and neglected her acting career. All while Richard slept with her friends, raged and fought with her in hotel rooms and publicly reproached her for her fluctuating weight. Their excessive, extravagant natures fueled each other, spiraling them both further into alcoholism, drug abuse and poor health.

Want to stay healthy? Don't walk, RUN from the Richard Burtons of the world. Surround yourself only with people who you consider in some way to be better, wiser, smarter, kinder or more educated than you or who possess some significant quality that inspires you to be a better person. In return, strive to give so much time to the improvement of yourself and your own life that you simply have no room for negative thoughts or time to spend with those who drag you down. This not only enhances your life and relationships but is also an act of deep self-love. When you surround yourself with quality people, your health, wealth and all of your relationships benefit.

Just like the food we choose, the people we choose to have in our lives are great contributors to our level of health.

5. Healthy is having a purpose in life

Hollywood lifestyles of the rich, famous and frequently idle, all too often lead to lives lacking contentment, purpose and the open search for deeper meaning. Actors so often become involved in causes not only because they are able to leverage their stardom for a good cause but because, deep down, we all need a purpose to feel happy and be healthy in life. And, well, acting alone isn't cutting it for most of them, as it didn't for Elizabeth Taylor.

In the end, according to long-time friend and designer Vicky Tiel, Elizabeth Taylor simply "wanted to be Earth Mother to her loved ones, to help the unfortunate ones...her generosity was her foremost quality." Perhaps due to the personal pain Elizabeth endured during her many and varied illnesses and stream of failed marriages, she empathized with those needing soothing, nurturing and loving. As Elizabeth matured, she began reaching out to those less fortunate. In addition to her own three children, she adopted a fourth and spent numerous hours, along with her hard earned dollars, on various humanitarian efforts. Her most famous effort being the incredible impact she made through her HIV/AIDS activism, raising more than $270 million and compassionate awareness during a time when the disease was highly stigmatized and very few stars would risk attaching their image to it.

Though riddled with ailments (she survived a reported 70 surgeries) and other complications from poor health habits, Elizabeth managed to live to the ripe age of 79. She ended her life surrounded by the things she loved most: a strong drink, good food and new friends. She rose to the accolades of

her peers through lifetime achievement
awards and countless events for
recognition of her contributions as
a charitable humanitarian. Noted by
Director George Cukor as possessing
"that rarest of virtues - simple kindness,"
she was also incredibly resilient. In the
end she showed the personal courage
to face the truth about her life and her
weight, confront her own demons and
address her hedonistic side ultimately
leading to a deeper health of spirit,
charity, and goodness for which she will
long be remembered.

Improve Your Health and Wellbeing with the Law of Autosuggestion

By Jim Thomas

Today, more than ever, researchers have advanced several theories regarding how the thought process affects health. Indeed, there's both theoretical and practical evidence that how you think affects your mental as well as physical health. Whether you find yourself in good health, or struggling with either acute or long-term health issues, you can use positive thinking through autosuggestion to bring better health and wellbeing into your life.

The Distinct Relationship Between Health and Psychology

Health and illness are influenced by a host of factors. In addition to contagious and hereditary illnesses and conditions that are common today, there are many behavioral and psychological factors that impact overall physical well-being and specific mental conditions. Health psychology is a discipline that focuses on understanding how biological, psychological, behavioral and social influences predetermine health and illness. An understanding of how this relationship works, and what exactly it entails, can be instrumental if you are trying to take advantage of proven mental tactics to cultivate positive health.

The field of health psychology is globally recognized, so much so that Division 38 of the American Psychological Association focuses exclusively on it. This division aims to understand health and illness, as well as to study the psychological aspects that influence health. Both illnesses and health can be seen as the result of a combination of biological, psychological and social factors. Biological factors include hereditary traits and genetic predispositions. On the other hand, psychological aspects that are commonly explored by this field include lifestyle, thought process, personality characteristics and stress levels. In the rest of this chapter, we're going to focus on a specific psychological factor referred to as autosuggestion and how it impacts health. You'll learn exactly how you can use autosuggestion to gain immense health benefits.

Understanding Autosuggestion

To understand autosuggestion, we'll first look at the meaning of suggestion in the psychological aspect. A suggestion is an intimation, idea, thought or something similar that's conveyed through the five physical senses (tasting, touching, smelling, seeing and hearing) or direct from mind to mind (telepathically). Autosuggestion is a suggestion to one's self by one's self. It's something you suggest to yourself.

Autosuggestion is about dominating the mind with thoughts in a way that impacts the subconscious mind. It's another way to communicate conscious thoughts so that they take control by summoning the subconscious mind. Simply put, it's about influencing the subconscious mind with thoughts that are either positive or negative.

Autosuggestion is a wildly popular technique, covered at great length by some of the world's most historical authors, including Napoleon Hill in his book 'Think and Grow Rich.' The mental technique of autosuggestion is influenced by hypnotism, which also focuses on gaining control of the subconscious mind. Autosuggestion has been successfully applied in numerous areas including educational undertakings, scientific approaches and psychological medicine. It's believed that man has no control over the things in his subconscious mind, which is essentially opposite from the belief that man always has control over his unconscious mind with the intervention of the five senses. Autosuggestion helps an individual to be in control over some very important aspects of his own being and existence, health included.

How Autosuggestion Works

Autosuggestion is employed as a medium to control one's self in which the subject voluntarily controls his subconscious mind with positive thoughts while at the same time ignoring any negative ones that may have an unwanted effect or outcome. As you might understand, the subconscious mind directly receives information from the conscious through the five physical senses. Interpretation of this information however varies from person to person, based on how the individual perceives it. This is where autosuggestion comes in to make sure that your perception of information from the conscious mind works toward enhancing your health benefits, rather than diminishing them. Over time, your perception of things subsides into your subconscious mind and eventually becomes part of what you believe in, influencing your actions.

Through effective application of autosuggestion, you can ensure that no negative or even positive thoughts set root in your subconscious mind without the conscious mind filtering them first. Therefore, the conscious mind acts as a guard or entry 'check point' before these thoughts can have any effect on your outlook and, thus, reality in life.

Autosuggestion at Work

You can effectively employ autosuggestion through a series of three simple steps:

The Power of 'I Am'

The use of self-affirmations like 'I Am' is the first step. Self-affirmations should be regularly repeated so that they can eventually sink into the subconscious mind and then turn into action. Positive thoughts ought to be considered in doing this especially when you're under a negative situation, health-related or otherwise. Although it's not a given that the negative situation will automatically disappear, one's perception of the situation will change the influence, thus belittling the negativity. For instance, uttering the sentence 'I am confident' regularly will become your reality.

Aligning Thoughts with the Right Emotions

As it happens, the subconscious mind cannot tell the difference between positive and negative thoughts. But it can sense the feeling of what is perceived, whether a fantasy or a reality. It's, therefore, necessary that you feed your mind with positive and uplifting thoughts mixed with desire and emotions – so that, eventually, the subconscious mind will turn them into action.

Repetition is Key

It's important that you state the positive statements aloud and often to channel them into your subconscious mind. As a rule of the thumb, say them aloud in the morning upon waking and in the evening before you go to bed. For instance, if you harbor a desire to gain a specific amount of money, state it out loud, and see and feel that you have it in your possession. This instructs your subconscious mind to have faith that you'll eventually obtain the amount of money that you so desire. Eventually, this becomes a habit. Through repetition, you will find this getting easier to do each day.

Using these simple steps, anyone can make use of autosuggestion to reap multiple health, mental and attitudinal benefits. A daily action plan for self-affirmations, or autosuggestions, is sufficient. Next, we look at fine tuning affirmations to actualize positive health.

Autosuggestion as a Way to Bolster Positive Health

To master the key principles underlying autosuggestive therapeutics, it's important that the physiological causes of disease are considered, or at least the very initial physiological stage of common health anomalies.

The most authoritative voices in the medical world argue that diseases are caused primarily by a failure of the cells to do their duty, or to repair their waste. It can be argued that there are mental causes behind this failure of the cells to do their duties, or to repair their waste for that matter. Some of the latest discoveries have ascertained the fact that there is a 'mind' in cells, with all the 'minds' in all the cells being connected to the subconscious mind by filaments. It follows then that anything that affects the subconscious mind can be said to affect the cells themselves, in varying degrees. Although this theory is considered a half-truth by researchers who simply believe there's more to it, the connection between the subconscious mind and the cell system in your body is a fact that cannot be understated.

Organic diseases can be influenced. It can be affirmed without hesitation that organic disorders come within the influence of autosuggestion. Although this observation might contradict the professional thinking of a number of doctors who rather judge the matter too harshly, it definitely makes sense practically. More doctors today are learning to embrace autosuggestion in their health practices and are, indeed, using it as a tool.

According to Emile Coue, a French practitioner who authored a book on Autosuggestion, solid evidence exists that positive affirmation can, indeed, eradicate diseases. Coue cites situations where French doctors used X-Rays and other forms of medical evidence to demonstrate autosuggestion at work. He cites an example where a young girl was afflicted with a fissure of the anus, and also had a tumor on the tenth rib. She had been ill for two years and in bed for three months. Her body temperature was running high and, generally, her condition was dire. The power of suggestion cured her within two weeks, with the tumor disappearing completely and the fissure healing without leaving a trace.

In some cases, medical doctors who leverage suggestion as a complementary tool in their work have found that symptoms can also completely disappear – without the illness going away. So the patient lives a normal life without having to suffer from the common effects of illnesses.

The number of illnesses - physical or mental - that can be cured through the power of autosuggestion are beyond the scope of this chapter. There's no limit to what can be accomplished with this 'law of attraction' technique. However, we'll look at a number of common illnesses that affect a lot of people today, and see how autosuggestion can come be used to gain some relief.

Autosuggestion has been shown to drastically improve symptoms and conditions related to diabetes, tuberculosis, sciatica, gastric problems, constipation, asthma and headaches. In addition to the absence of symptoms, wasted tissue has also been shown to repair.

Another area where autosuggestion has been practiced for ages, and with great results, is beauty (used by men and women to enhance their good looks). Whether it's to smooth away those impertinent wrinkles, repair sagging cheeks or just restore the laughing sparkle to dulled eyes, autosuggestion leads to positive change. The idea is to train your imagination to visualize your face or body the way you would like it to be, and you'll have a very good chance of approaching your ideal.

Examples of Useful Health Affirmations

When it comes to positive health affirmations, there is no limit. You can accomplish just about all your health-related desires and goals by creating affirmations that positively act against negative situations. Just make sure you are repeating your affirmations often and aloud. Here are a number of common health affirmations that have successfully improved health:

- Every day in every way I'm getting healthier and healthier and feeling better and better.

- I love myself and I'm perfectly healthy.

- Every single cell in my body is health conscious. I am a health freak.

- I am full of energy and vitality and my mind is calm and peaceful.

- I avoid junk food. I eat healthy, nutritious food that benefits my body and large quantities of water that cleanses my body.

- I think only positive thoughts and I am always happy and joyous, no matter what the external conditions are.

- Every day is a new day full of hope,

happiness and health.

- I am free of diabetes, free of blood pressure problems and free of all life-threatening diseases.

- Sit down and create a list of your own affirmations that align with your health goals. Say them out loud, repeatedly, and they will become your health reality!

Conclusion

It's very important to note that autosuggestion works together with the ordinary rules of good health. If you are looking to get rid of a certain condition through autosuggestion, while at the same time consuming the same foods that caused the condition, it won't work. Lead a health-rational life. Incorporate sufficient exercise and a healthy diet to your daily life. A doctor is also a necessity. Practice autosuggestion in line with professional medical help. Most importantly, TAKE ACTION. Autosuggestion works when practiced in conjunction with action. So sail away from the conventional mindset, embrace autosuggestion and gradually watch your health soar to its optimal state..

Filling My Own Tank
How I Stayed Healthy and Balanced While Caring For a Loved One

By Mia Staysko

We knew it was coming. After all, my father-in-law Bob had turned 88 in June and my mother-in-law Joyce was not far behind at 84. We had tried to convince them to downsize from their two-story home into something smaller, preferably a supportive living residence that at least had the option for assistance if, and when, they needed it. Our efforts were met with fierce resistance. So, with the knowledge that something tragic would likely be the ultimate motivator, we honored their decisions and did our best to assist. We took over the driving to medical appointments, helped out with the household chores and did our best to be supportive. And then it happened.

Early one morning, Joyce called to say
that Bob had fallen during the middle of
the night and she had been unable to get
him back up on his feet. They had waited
until morning to call for help and she had
stoically made him as comfortable on the
floor as she could until then. Bob had been
getting thinner and thinner and had recently
been diagnosed with lymphoma in his right
eye. Now, here he was lying on the floor,
too weak to lift himself back to upright.

The days and weeks following became a
blur. The thing we had all dreaded had
happened and, as he was hospitalized, it
became increasingly clear that not only was
Bob going to need ongoing care, but Joyce
was also unable to be alone. Though we
knew she had dementia, we were suddenly
made aware of the severity of the situation
and it was decided that she should not,
could not, stay in her home. She came to
our house to live until we could figure out

what the next move was going to be. We had instantly become primary caregivers for Joyce and primary decision makers for Bob.

To be more accurate, I had become the primary caregiver with my husband Steve playing a supporting role. Being self-employed with a home office meant that I would put my business on hold in order to look after the myriad of details and decisions that would need to be made both for Bob and for Joyce in the near future. Luckily for us, neither of our two boys was living at home at this time. With one working in another city and one away at college, we would be able to focus on looking after Bob and Joyce. Many are not so lucky and are asked to assist with elderly parents while still caring full-time for their young children.

Taking a family member into your own home, or even caring for someone who becomes ill within your own household, or offering to help a friend going through medical treatment can be a very stressful endeavor. No matter how much you love the person you are helping, it can drain you physically, mentally and emotionally. It can also put tremendous strain on your relationships, both with the person you are caring for and with everyone around you. And while the needs of others seem most pressing, at a time like this it is essential to care for yourself and to remember that you and your needs are also important. You cannot care for another without first caring for yourself. Like the classic airline safety demonstration, you've got to get your own oxygen mask on, make sure you are going to survive, before you can help anyone else.

Sometimes fatigue and stress can kind of sneak up on us. We think that visiting a friend in the hospital or running errands for them feels easy. After all, it isn't that far out of our normal routine. However, we are still extending ourselves and lending our energy out to others. That is a wonderful and loving thing to do, but we need to remember that if we keep spending our energy without ever filling ourselves back up, we are going to end up with a deficit. We've got to be able to replenish our own energy reserves.

Hospitals and medical centers are stressful places, even if you are just the visitor or if you are accompanying someone else. Simply going to visit a friend for an hour or so or lounging in the waiting room can be surprisingly draining. Doing these things for an extended period of time can be downright exhausting.

Caregiver stress is widely recognized in the medical community, and is known to actually increase the potential for illness in those who are simply doing their best to help and support their loved ones. So how does one remain healthy and balanced while providing tender loving care to another? Here's what worked for me.

Knowing Myself

I have a pretty good handle on my own body, mind and spirit and what my normal feels like. So as soon as something feels out of sorts, I pay attention. Understanding that I function best with eight hours of sleep and that I also need to move my body gently but regularly all played a part in understanding when I wasn't feeling at my best. It didn't always help me to get what I needed but at least it helped me to know what it was and then to work on that.

Being Flexible

Sleep is generally never an issue for me. I get between 7 and 8 hours of uninterrupted sleep pretty much every night. This was one area though that went a bit out of whack while caring for my in-laws. The stress of having someone in my home for an extended period of time, along with the stress of having to help with some really challenging decisions on my father-in-law's behalf, both before and after his passing, definitely affected my sleep.

My daily routines were already turned upside down so allowing myself to go with the flow and do whatever needed to be done today in whatever order presented itself, helped me to not get completely stressed out.

I took advantage of the down time that was available when Joyce napped in the afternoons to get some of my needs met. I made phone calls, checked in on my business needs and volunteer duties, went outside for a quick walk or napped myself to fill out my sleep deficit. My daily routines were turned upside down anyway, so allowing myself to go with the flow and do whatever needed to be done today in whatever order presented itself reduced my stress.

Honoring My Energetic Type

Knowing, for example, that I am an introvert who needs to have time alone in order to recharge, meant that I made sure that hubby took over at the end of the day. I imagine this would be a whole lot more challenging for extroverts who require fun and social interaction to be at their best, as that would have required physically getting out of the house. For me, allowing myself time for a phone call with friends or catching up through social media was enough of a lifeline to the outside world.

Staying Physically Active
As Best I Could

Exercise is important at all times and being

one of the best known stress relievers, it is
even more important to get moving when
providing care to another. Unfortunately,
it can also be another difficult need to
fill, as getting away, or finding the time,
can be a real challenge. Personally, if I
had to choose between picking up the dry
cleaning and getting myself to a yoga class
or taking the dog for a quick walk while
Grandma was napping, moving my body
won. If our situation had been longer
term, I would have had to come up with a
more comprehensive strategy for this one
and may have had to use that flexibility
quality to go to a gym at night, not my
favorite time to exercise.

Breathing

I love breathing! It is the simplest tool
I know of to reduce stress and increase
health, and I have to do it anyway so why
not include it in my tools for balancing my
health? Breathing fully and consciously is a

great way to get in touch with reality, to get yourself out of the past, or future, to be present for a moment or two. It can help you to stay calm when making challenging decisions or when in environments that feel stressful. I highly recommend becoming friends with your own breath.

Making Time for Relationships

Lack of privacy was a real issue for us while Joyce was in our home. I would sneak outside or wait for her to take a nap to make phone calls to friends. This became tiring quickly and was a real strain. I felt bad for sneaking around, but the reality was that this was what was going on in my day-to-day life so it meant that while chatting with a friend, I felt like I was talking about her behind her back. I needed the support from my friends just as much as my in-laws needed our support and running off to a quick coffee with a girlfriend wasn't an option.

Steve and I also had to figure out how to stay connected and united. Physical and emotional intimacy is not exactly easy with your mommy in the house and this was one area that was only addressed by asking for respite. We were lucky to have other family members who lived nearby. They would take Joyce for the occasional weekend so that we could have some time to recharge our relationship and return, at least for a time, to some sense of normalcy. I had no idea how much I appreciated our quiet time together and in the bigger picture, the contrast made our connection stronger.

Asking Myself
"What Do I Need Right Now?"

If you find yourself, like we did, in the position of caring for another, either short term or long term and you are finding it to be stressful, ask yourself "Is it my mind, my body or my spirit that most needs my attention right now?" Whatever that answer is, just do that, even if it is just for a moment. If you feel like hiding in a closet, it may be that your spirit needs silence. If you are anxious and edgy, your body may be asking for a stretch or a run. If you are tired, sneak in a nap. Tuning in to your own needs is an essential part of remaining healthy while looking after someone else.

In the bigger picture, we were very lucky. Our parents have the resources to be able to afford good housing and care, meaning that our toe-dip into the world of caring for the elderly was temporary, at least for now. So many people do not have it so lucky. As the boomers continue to age, there will likely be entire generations of people who will be forced to put their own needs on the back burner in order to support their loved ones.

In the long run, as is the way with most things, there were both good and bad things about taking on the responsibility of looking after Joyce for a time. Despite the challenges, the lack of sleep due to added stress and the loss of privacy, it was our honor, and, we felt our duty, to help out this lovely woman who raised my husband. The time together brought us closer at a time when increasing memory loss will eventually create a wider rift.

We were also better able to observe and understand Joyce's needs, both medically and functionally, for the near future. This allowed us to confidently find suitable housing for her and to feel comfortable that she can handle a certain amount of independence, at least for now. We have our home and our time back to ourselves. This experience has offered us a little glimpse into our own potential aging picture as well, reminding us to do whatever it takes to remain mobile, mentally alert and healthy.

I, for one, will be eating my veggies!

Being Healthy in an Unhealthy World
Wisdom from an ancient philosopher

By Angi Ma Wong

Those of you who are familiar with my work have seen one of my favorite quotes by Confucius in my other publications. I always thought it would be the ideal saying to put at the main entrance of every school so all who entered, both children and adults alike, could read and remember its message in their hearts.

> *If there is light in the soul,*
> *there is beauty in the person.*
> *If there is beauty in the person,*
> *there is harmony at home.*
> *If there is harmony at home,*
> *there is order in the nation.*
> *If there is order in the nation,*
> *there is peace in the world.*
> –Confucius

I bring it up here because I believe that it is the heart of this book about health and happiness. For your mental and physical health, seek the light—that is SUNlight, which the body converts to Vitamin D when it hits our skin.

As we age, we tend to lose the body fat that keeps us warm, so we put on hats and long sleeves, and stay indoors, thus depriving ourselves of vital Vitamin D, which gives us energy, boosts our immune systems, keeps our moods in balance, and enhances our bone health. Even younger folks aren't getting enough of this essential vitamin, because they mostly work indoors and use sunscreen when outdoors.

People who have the lowest levels of Vitamin D are 40% more likely to catch colds and flu. Those who take daily supplements of at least 800 to 1200 IU of Vitamin D a day lower the number of colds or flu they experience.

Unfortunately, widespread avoidance of the sun due to fear of skin cancer, which occurs from over-exposure, has resulted in a decrease of Vitamin D in our average blood levels, according to a report in the Archives of Internal Medicine, which was featured in the 2009 September/October issue of AARP magazine. The same article states that Vitamin D's benefits include reduced risks for cancer (at least six different types), heart disease (especially in men), hip fractures, and tooth loss and an increase in muscle strength.

So, get outside and soak in the sun! Better yet, walk for at least a half hour daily, either in ten-minute increments or all thirty minutes at once, but however you do it, try to expose your bare skin to at least 10–20 minutes of sunshine daily if you can. Both the oxygen that you inhale and the Vitamin D that your body makes when sunlight hits your body's largest organ (the skin), are powerful allies on your path to better health.

Get (back) in Touch with Nature

In the manic hustle and bustle of 21st century life in which we are surrounded by science, technology, computers, mobile and cell devices and electronic communication, exercise and a routine of being outdoors energize me every morning. It gives me the feeling of being grounded each day and prepares me mentally and physically for the day ahead. Combining your exercise with communing with nature is a great way to reap the rewards of both.

My daily walk is something that I am religious about. It began fifteen years ago after I took a free test at a Rotary-sponsored health fair and discovered that my cholesterol levels were higher than normal. The discovery impelled me to launch a daily routine that now starts my day. Being a morning person, I find that getting up and out right away best fits my natural body clock and lifestyle before my day becomes too busy. An added benefit is that the exercise clears my mind and generates new energy, as well as stimulates creative thoughts and ideas, so I carry a pen and pad in my pocket to jot them down.

Only you can choose the most convenient time and that is the one decision key to adhering to any exercise program. Whether you're an early bird or a night owl, get out and moving and back to nature by at least walking or biking at least half an hour daily, five days a week.

If you can't fit in a solid half hour, break it into three 10-minute workouts. Step out of your office and walk outside, around your building, away from your desk and the computer for ten minutes. Hold your head and shoulders straight with your tummy tucked in, and swing your arms as you breathe deeply from your diaphragm.

Women over 50 who either ride their bicycles or walk moderately 45 minutes a day for five or more days a week only contract colds 30% of the time, compared to the 50% of women who exercise only by stretching once a week. Initially, it takes exercising seven days a week to lose weight and five days a week to maintain those lost pounds.

You'll be increasing the oxygen and blood flowing throughout your body, speeding up your food absorption, getting nutrients out to your cells, strengthening your heart and many other muscles, preventing a stroke or heart attack and decreasing stress hormones.

The best thing about walking is that it's free, except for an investment in a comfortable pair of walking shoes. Two pairs are better so that they can be worn alternately, allowing each to dry out. You don't need to drive to and from a gym or health club, pay membership fees or keep up with or spend on the latest in exercise fashions. You don't have to share equipment handled and touched by countless other people who have left behind their germs and sweat. You won't expose yourself to showers, floors, lockers and other facilities shared by who knows how many strangers. Moreover, there is an entire branch of traditional Chinese medicine dedicated to reflexology, based on the belief that all of our body's organs and functions are activated through the acupressure points located on the bottoms of our feet. When we walk, we are literally and actively contributing to our own good health and well-being.

Imagine that with every breath and step you take, your immune system is getting a boost, not to mention your overall health. Don't be surprised to find your cholesterol level and blood pressure lowered, your diabetes and weight tamed, your emotions in better control and your feeling of general well-being enhanced immensely.

If walking doesn't appeal to you, swim, bicycle, shoot hoops with your kids, push the old-fashioned lawn mower across your yard or the mop and vacuum inside your home, garden, dance, even wash windows. All of these can give your body the workout it needs to keep in shape as you stretch, reach and pull your muscles. Whatever activity you choose, keep active to burn up the calories.

Remember to warm up before, and cool down after, you exercise. Eat a snack that has both a carbohydrate and a protein within 15 minutes after working out so your body can transform your food into muscle-healing glycogen. Your body, mind and spirit will all thank you!

Nature is painting for us, day after day, pictures of infinite beauty if only we have the eyes to see them.
–John Ruskin

Old is New Again

I grew up with, and am a passionate
believer in, the philosophy that is the
foundation of traditional Chinese medicine
(TCM) to prevent illness and disease
naturally. It works through following
a good diet that boosts my body's
regenerative and recuperation powers from
inside out, coupled with exercise and a
balanced lifestyle. TCM is based on the
profound belief in the mind-body-spirit
connection that has been known and
practiced in China for thousands of years,
long before Western medicine developed.

The major difference is that TCM has
always focused on treating the whole
person, connecting the mind, body and
spirit, and emphasized preventing illness
and disease in the first place, not just curing
the symptoms as does Western medicine.
The three core tenets of TCM (and feng
shui, acupuncture, acupressure, reflexology,

meditation, martial arts, tai chi, chi gong, herbal and folk cures) are: the flow of vital energy (chi), the five elements (wood, fire, earth, metal, water), and the balance between yin (female, nurturing, dark, quiet) and yang (male, aggressive, light, active). To the Chinese way of thinking, culture and life, these three integral components determine the state of our health, well-being, relationships, and ultimately, our lives and longevity. Many of our health challenges today originate from our lifestyles, diets or emotions.

Because the basic philosophy of TCM is so vastly different from Western traditional medicine's methods of curing sickness and disease, it has taken over a generation for it to be accepted in the United States by health professionals and mainstream America. And yet for thousands of years, Chinese traditional medicine has been well documented and practiced throughout the history of the world's oldest continuous civilization.

It is holistic, natural and integrated, utilizing what is provided to us in the form of organic material such as plants, flowers, trees, roots, vegetables, fruits, herbs, spices and even animals. On the other hand, most Western medicines are synthetic, developed by pharmaceutical companies.

Chinese tradition teaches us to eat appropriately to maintain balance in our lives and to prevent disease and illness in our bodies, spirits and minds. Even our meals are cooked to include the five flavors: sweet, salty, bitter, sour and pungent; and every food is designated as being either yin or yang and having either cold or hot energy.

Each of those same elements is associated with an emotion, a major organ or system within our bodies, a taste, a compass direction, a number, an animal symbol, a color and many aspects of our lives.

Heart problems? Bring more joy and laughter into your life. Liver or vision problems? Manage your anger and frustration. Have trouble breathing or something wrong with your respiratory system or lungs? Get grief counseling right away. Stomach, weight or digestive illness? Take measures to stop worry and stress, which research has shown causes you to overeat, neglect exercise and sound eating habits and gain weight. Kidneys or hearing malfunctioning? Face your fears.

We meditate and savor quiet time and serenity to bring peace to our minds, bodies and spirits. We balance life with joy and activity, working hard and exercising. We nourish and enrich ourselves with knowledge, satisfying and loving, familial relationships and strong faith systems. We accept that life is a integral part of a grand universe as well as nature, both of which move in cycles of birth and death, to repeat over and over through time.

Thanks to modern technology, the Internet and the old standby, books and libraries, information is readily available to all of us. We have free choice to empower ourselves and take charge of our health.

Your First Drink of the Day

Water is essential to all life on and the life of our planet. It is probably the most precious resource that we have. Every creature or plant that has ever existed here required water, either to drink it or live in it. Wars have been waged and lives in both the animal and plant kingdoms have been lost to obtain water, its access or its source.

We humans can live without food for seven days, but would perish if we did without this elixir of life for three days. It doesn't take much imagination to understand that without good old H2O, there would be no life on earth and it would be as barren as the moon.

Here's how critical water is to the proper functioning of our bodies. It makes up 83% of our blood, 75% of our brain and muscles and 22% of our bones. Water is the conduit that removes waste, transports and aids in the absorption of oxygen and nutrients from our food to our bodies, prepares oxygen so we can breathe it, protects our organs and joints and keeps our bodies at an even temperature.

Both my Uncle Arthur and his wife Edna, who were both physicians, gave me the following advice:

- Take your first drink after you wake up in the morning upon arising from a good night's sleep. The first thing that should enter your system is warm, filtered water within the hour. This habit is practiced by many people in Asia, especially in Japan, to aid in food absorption, to get their bodies' "plumbing" activated by stimulating their intestines and to help flush out the waste produced in their bodies while they were sleeping.

Drink between two to four glasses of warm water on an empty stomach first thing in the morning, and then brush your teeth, clean your mouth and do not take any food or water for 45 minutes.

I find that break to be the ideal time to go on my morning walk and return home in time to eat my breakfast within the hour of my rising. That water will hydrate your body and keep your kidneys and liver in good working order, as well as keep your skin clear and your mind and spirit soothed as you commune with nature.

- Invest in a water filter for your kitchen faucet, either under-the-sink or a removable one on a pitcher. Filtering your water removes the carcinogens before you drink it. You can also add freshly-squeezed lemon juice to help maintain your pH balance at the beginning of the day. You can also drink a cinnamon (1 teaspoon)-honey (1 tablespoon)-apple cider vinegar (2 tablespoons) mixture that is dissolved in warm water, or sip a cup of non-caffeinated herbal or green tea before breakfast. Any of these drinks is gentle on your stomach, natural and healthy during your day, as well.

While you may not think of yourself as a plant, here's a daily human "irrigation schedule" to maintain for good health:

- Two glasses of water upon rising for your internal organs

- One glass of water a half hour before meals to aid digestion and help weight loss by feeling full

- One glass of water before your bath or shower to lower your blood pressure

- One glass of water before retiring for the night to help your blood circulation, which helps to avoid heart attacks and strokes.

- Water is priceless. Use it wisely and prudently, and treat it as the treasure it is to yourself and the planet.

The sun shines not on us, but in us.
-John Muir

Examining a Food Label

In January 2009, Dr. Mehmet Oz was a guest on the Oprah Winfrey show and revealed five ingredients we should watch out for in packaged foods. While I did not see the show, the information was shared with me by a receptionist at my oncologist's office and I added it to a little card I carry in my wallet.

Don't purchase or eat any product that has any of the following words listed among the first five ingredients on a food label:

1. Sugar
2. High fructose corn syrup
3. Enriched wheat flour
4. Saturated (animal) fat
5. Hydrogenated oil

Federal law requires that ingredients on every food label must be listed in order by the amount used to make whatever is in a processed food. Quite simply, it means that when you see sugar listed first after the word "Ingredients" on a package, there is more sugar than anything else in the food inside, followed by the second ingredient, then the third.

If you see "enriched wheat flour" listed first among the ingredients on the wrapping on a loaf of bread, don't be fooled or misled as many of us (myself included) have been. The word "enriched" means that the wheat flour has been processed, e.g., bleached, or has additives of some sort included. It does not mean nutritious ingredients have been added to the wheat flour, the main ingredient used to make that bread.

More often than not, other common descriptions, such as those listed below, can be very misleading:

- Good source of whole grains
- Organic
- Sugar-free
- High fiber

For an experiment, go to the bread section of your grocer or a health food store. Pick up several similar types of bread from different companies, for example, compare five or six different loaves of "wheat bread," "multi-grain bread" or whatever kind you enjoy or usually purchase.

Read and compare the labels and make note of the order in which the ingredients are listed, remembering that the quantity of any ingredient puts it closer to the head of the list. A simple comparison will reveal how much sugar, sugar substitutes and other artificial sweeteners, preservatives, salt and other things such as high fructose corn syrup are included.

Check everything on that label, including the number of calories, amount of sodium and other nutrients on any packaged food you buy. This custom will also help you to identify anything to which you may be allergic, such as milk, soy, eggs, peanuts, wheat, fish, coconut and shellfish.

Did you ever notice how many grams of sodium can be found in the following items: a can of V-8 juice (which you can duplicate by substituting a can of tomato juice and adding hot sauce, celery juice or stalk and pepper to taste) or soup, a tub of cottage cheese, a package of chips or miso soup or in a baking mix or other processed food? At the cost of 150,000 deaths and $24 billion a year in the United States, salt consumption has resulted in an alarming increase in strokes, heart disease and hypertension.

If we are to keep to a healthy 2000-calorie-a-day diet, but we're not careful, we can consume between 400 and 1,500 mg of sodium and one to three days' amount of saturated fat by eating a box of popcorn from the movie concession stand, according to www.WebMD.com.

Don't overlook the amount of the different kinds of fat, such as artery-clogging saturated fat, trans fat, and cholesterol. These bad fats are found in red meat; whole-milk dairy products such as ice cream, butter, cheese, and sour cream; creamy sauces and dressings; anything fried; palm and palm kernel oil, cocoa butter, peanut and coconut oil (although great for moisturizing your skin) and lard.

Good fats are monounsaturated, such as olive, canola, argan and grape seed oils and, unlike saturated fats, do not become solid at room temperature. Take another look at the small print of the ingredients in that protein powder or bar that you eat and you may be shocked. By the way, if you are paying more for more protein in a protein drink, shake or food, think again. Your body can only process 5 to 9 grams of protein an hour, so if that canned or bottled shake has 43 grams listed, for example, 34 grams and your money literally goes down the toilet as it is eliminated from your body.

Developing a habit of religiously reading food labels is one of the best things you can immediately begin doing for yourself and your family. You will save money and time on doctors, tests, lab work and hospital bills later as you prevent health problems.

Country Diets Versus City Diets

The story about Professor Janet Plant also came to me through an email. She is a scientist from the United Kingdom who was treated five times for cancer with radiotherapy and chemotherapy.

Her husband's well-meaning Chinese friends had sent to him cards, messages and herbal suppositories during a trip to take to Plant as cures for her breast cancer. The couple, both scientists, got into a discussion and were curious as to why women in China had practically non-existent incidences of cancer.

The proverbial light bulb went off when both Dr. Plant and her husband realized at about the same time, that Chinese women did not consume dairy products. The Chinese diet in the 1980s showed only 14% of the caloric intake was from fat, while the Western diet indicated 34% was from fat. The Chinese diet did not include cow's milk, cheese, ice cream or yogurt; nor were any of these fed to their babies.

Statistics indicated that Chinese women in general only got cancer at the rate of 1 in 10,000; in Hong Kong, 1 in 34; and in the United Kingdom, the ratio was 1 in 12. Even in the aftermath of the atomic attacks on Hiroshima and Nagasaki, the incidence was still only half of that of Western women living in industrial cities.

When I read Dr. Plant's article, I remembered

something that had happened to me over 20 years ago when I had my first cancer experience. My oncologist commented that he could think of only one reason why I was the first and only one of four sisters to get cancer, as there was no history of it in my parents or my family. He speculated that it was because I had been adopted at six months old into the Ma family and had spent my childhood growing up in New Zealand.

When I heard Dr. Link say that, it made perfect sense. During my childhood, I grew up eating lots of red meat in the form of lamb and drank milk that was delivered to our home in bottles with an inch of cream at the top. Moreover, I had reached puberty in Taiwan early at the age of eleven and breast fed my children, two other conditions that put me on the high-risk category to get breast cancer. On the other hand, my three sisters had grown up in China and Taiwan where eating beef, cheese and yogurt and drinking milk were not common in their Chinese diets.

The Japanese-American radiologist at St. John's Medical Center in Santa Monica gave me some alarming statistics when my first tumor was discovered in 1989. Japanese women only developed breast cancer at the rate of 1 in 4,000 and American women were getting it at the rate of 1 in 11.

But the ratio for fourth-generation American women of Japanese descent was 1 in 8. His opinion was that lifestyle and diet were the culprits. (Unfortunately, today's breast cancer rate among non-Asian women in the United States has caught up to 1 in 8.)

In Hong Kong, a British colony for ninety-nine years, the breast cancer rate among women is 1 in 34, especially among the more affluent. That figure is traced to eating a primarily Western diet richer in fats, red meat and dairy products, in sharp contrast to the far healthier diets of Chinese women.

The latter's meals remain predominantly comprised of vegetables, fish, chicken, rice, soups and some pork, typically the traditional foods of southern Chinese provinces. Moreover, most of the women in China still worked in rural areas outdoors in contrast to the Hong Kong residents, who lived and worked in high-density factories and office buildings in Hong Kong and Kowloon's countless high rises.

Dr. Plant eliminated beef and dairy products from her diet and monitored her tumor, which began to shrink within a very short time.

When to Eat What at Each Meal

I don't remember where I picked up this tip, but after some thought about our digestive systems, it was another strategy that really made a lot of sense. At meals, eat the protein first, then the vegetables. This practice is more natural and in tune with how your body digests your food.

You should eat protein at the beginning of your meal because it takes about twenty-four hours to digest in your body. Following it up with your vegetables which have all-important fiber helps your body process food along your interior plumbing more efficiently.

The French got it right by eating their salad at the end of a meal, while the Chinese traditionally serve hot soups or fresh fruit for dessert instead of cakes, ice cream, pies and other sweets loaded with carbohydrates, sugar and calories.

A good analogy is how you wash your dishes—in hot, soapy water to cut the grease on your dinnerware, cooking and eating utensils, getting everything squeaky clean. Those hot liquids, including water and tea, assist your body in breaking down the fats you have consumed, and move them out of your body.

Get into the SPSP Habit

At the same time I was nibbling throughout the day, staving off hunger, I also put myself on the SPSP diet. SPSP stands for Smaller Portion, Smaller Plate. In the West, we tend to eat our food served from large-sized plates and fill the plate up.

The food industry has been steadily increasing the sizes of meals for many years and unconsciously, also our caloric intake, resulting in the alarming explosion of obesity, both in children and adults.

If your parents were like mine, survivors of the Depression era, they urged us to clean up our plates so as not to waste food. Remember being told, "Think of the starving children in ____(fill in the country, usually China)." So being obedient children, we obeyed.

Consider a new way of eating your meals by using smaller plates, such as salad size, especially in the evening. You can still fill up your plate so you don't feel deprived, but common sense says that you will only be consuming less.

If you wish to grow thinner, diminish your dinner,
And take to light claret, instead of pale ale.
– H.S. Leigh

If you shove your food into your mouth, wolfing it down and barely chewing each bite, you will have consumed a larger quantity in the first twenty minutes than if you had eaten more slowly and enjoyed your meal. It takes that amount of time for the stomach to relay the message to your brain that it is full. Everything you eat afterward is over-eating.

Take your time to eat slowly and chew your food thoroughly (33 chews to each bite) and put down your fork in between bites. Relax and savor the flavors. Let your 10,000 taste buds do their work so you can truly appreciate your meals.

If you have difficulty slowing your pace, try eating spicy food. You'll be forced to take smaller bites, breathe or drink water and, by the way, heavily-seasoned foods speed up your metabolism.

You'll be doing your stomach a big favor by helping it to break down what you eat so that your body can use it for absorption, healing, energy, regeneration and growth. Twenty minutes into the meal, you will begin to feel full. That's your signal to stop eating.

One more tip: Use blue-colored plates. Some people found that the color blue makes food less appetizing and you may tend to eat less.

Eat Seasonal Foods

To live a balanced life, one needs to be aware of the cycles of nature and follow their flow. In nutrition, this means practicing the Chinese tradition of eating seasonal foods to align your body with nature's rhythms and the five elements: spring (wood), summer (fire), late summer (earth), autumn (metal), winter (water). Each of these also represents the major organs that we must nourish and keep at their top efficiency: the liver, heart, stomach, lungs and kidneys.

Take your cue on what to eat from your local farmer's market or grocery store produce section and avail yourself of the cornucopia that awaits you. Drink lots of water year-round, regardless of the season.

Spring

Spring in almost every culture around the

world represents new life, new growth and new beginnings. It is a time of rebirth and renewal after winter's rest. We begin to look and see with fresh eyes and perspectives, feel rejuvenated and hopeful, and look into ourselves and perhaps even experience transformation.

This is the time to eat lightly, to rid yourself and your body of waste and fat, shunning heavy, salty foods and seasonings. Beets, carrots, fresh greens, all kinds of sprouts, legumes, garlic, onions, seeds, grains, and cereal grasses such as wheat and barley can be seasoned with fragrant herbs such as rosemary, dill, basil and bay leaf. The best way to cook your food in the spring is to stir-fry it, using high heat and very little cooking oil.

Try to eat a little bit of raw food daily to strengthen your liver, which is the organ that is responsible for most of the detoxification in your body. A well-functioning liver is reflected in a calm person who does not become easily stressed or tense.

Summer

Summer is a time of outward strength and activity, expansion and development, creativity and light, growth, joy and productivity. It is a time to enjoy the abundance of life, whether it is from soaking in the sun's rays or partaking of the fruits and vegetables that are bursting with color and variety during this season.

Serve lighter and smaller meals that cool the body and lighten and boost your heart's health, especially with fresh vegetable or fruit salads, cucumbers, apples, lemons and celery. Drink flower teas, such as Chinese chrysanthemum (try this drink after it has cooled and sweeten with a small amount of honey) or Western chamomile, lemongrass or mint with lime.

Fill your grocery cart with lettuce and sprouts such as soy, alfalfa and mung bean. Add all summer fruits such as peaches, strawberries and nectarines, which fill the shelves at this time of year. Season your food with spices that are heat-generating, as the resultant perspiration helps to eliminate waste from your body through your skin as well as cool it.

Avoid heavy foods such as seeds, meats and dairy products,   nuts or grains, all of which can make you lethargic. Minimize the use of refined sugar, coffee, refined salt and flour, and tobacco. And in "the good ole summertime," watermelon is believed to have a wonderfully cooling, cleansing effect inside your body. The light summer soups made with the white part of melons found just under the rinds are prized for their liver-boosting qualities.

Late in the summer, a subtle change starts taking place as we and the earth prepare ourselves for a change in the seasons. This is the time to aid your stomach and digestive system in its transition to heavier foods.

Meals should still be light without heavy seasonings, and the best ingredients are those that are yellow or orange in color or round in shape. All are believed to help us to stay grounded and include corn, beans of all kinds (especially soy and garbanzo), millet, cabbage, cantaloupe, yams and sweet potatoes, long and string beans, peas, black beans, squash, zucchini, pumpkin, oats, potatoes and apricots.

Fall (Autumn)

Autumn is the time of harvest around the globe—a time to put aside food and store it for the coming colder months, to dress in warmer clothing and begin planning for the oncoming, less productive months of winter.

We, the earth and nature together start pulling ourselves inward, even as all three store energy in various ways. The season of fall is related to the lungs and involves consuming more sour and fermented foods such as those that have been salted or pickled (but only in small quantities), which cause us to contract just as we inhale to breathe or to "pucker up."

Food and drinks that are appropriate during this season include soy and almond milk, barley and millet, apples, peanuts, seaweed, pine nuts, shellfish such as crab, clams, oysters and mussels, rice and rice porridge, mushrooms, daikon radishes, turnips, red radishes, watercress, chard, cauliflower, spinach, pears, papaya and persimmons.

Winter

Winter approaches and both the earth and we prepare to rest, storing up fat and energy to see us through this season. It is the time to focus on the kidneys, and consume foods that enhance our appetite. Salty and bitter are the tastes for this time of year. Ideal foods are: vegetable soups with lots of celery, turnips and carrots, as well as other foods such as sweet rice, watercress, bitter melon, quinoa, oats, alfalfa, most kinds of beans, asparagus, winter squash, cranberries, melons, chlorella, wheat berry, ginger, seaweed, fennel, water chestnut, various berries and foods with omega-3 fatty acids.

With the cold and flu season predictable each winter, start helping your body to fight back. Eat more mushrooms of any kind, fatty fish such as salmon, mackerel or herring, and lots of garlic, using up to three fresh cloves daily in your cooking or even taking garlic in capsule form. This ancient food helps your body to fight the first signs of a cold. Drink up to five cups of green or black tea a day for two weeks to stave off flu and cold germs.

Watch What you put on your Skin

Whether you shower or bathe at night or in the morning, be careful what you put on your skin, which is the largest organ of your body. Convert to using only natural products, especially those that have fewer chemicals. Read the ingredients listed on the labels of your soap, shampoo, conditioner, foundation and other cosmetics, lotions, creams and so on. Remember that anything that you put on your skin will be absorbed into your body.

Notice that most of the ingredients are man-made chemicals with names you cannot pronounce nor do you know what they are. Moreover, the majority of skin care products have a list of ingredients that often cover a good portion of the container. Start looking for and using products that contain five or fewer natural ingredients.

Read the labels religiously and shun any skin, hair or nail product that has more than five ingredients listed. Think about Pacific Islander inhabitants who cook with locally-available coconut oil, or the folks in Mediterranean countries who have used olive, grape seed and argan oil for centuries in both geographic regions for their cooking and on their skin, hair and nails.

You can store these oils in larger bottles in your refrigerator after opening to prevent spoilage, and pour out a small amount to keep handy for smoothing right onto your skin after you bathe or shower, as they are easily absorbed.

Over 30 years ago, there were already books available that preached, "If you wouldn't put it in your mouth and eat it, don't put it on your skin." It made much good sense then and applies even more so today, three decades and tens of thousands of new chemicals later.

So many current choices in bath, bed, eye, hair, skin, hair and body products have been created from a plethora of synthetic substances, it is no wonder that there is an alarming increase of all sorts of skin disorders, allergies, illnesses and cancers.

Through technology today, you can easily access information on how to make your own skin care products from fruits and vegetables. Make small quantities when you are preparing your meals and keep them refrigerated in a glass jar until ready for use. How more chemical-free and natural can you get?

For generations, slices of cucumbers have been used to reduce puffiness in and around the eyes. Coconut, grape seed and olive oil can be smoothed right onto your skin after a bath or washing your face or hands. Avocado or yogurt can be face masks. Lemon juice can lighten your hair. I myself spread leftover egg white straight from the shell right onto my face and neck to firm my skin.

Cantaloupe, papaya, strawberry, tomato, potato, peach, watercress, watermelon, rose, walnut, sunflower, saffron, turmeric, sandalwood and countless other natural ingredients help to keep you healthy from inside, by eating them often, and outside, by applying them on your skin.

Other Health Tips:

- Use natural cleaning products

- Remove toxins from your home and workplace as much as you can: chemical, electronic, human, environmental, air, electrical

- Keep your home and work space germ-free

- Be vigilant about your personal health habits in public places, especially hotels and airplanes.

What's Love Got To Do With It?

By Kim Klein

"A wise physician once said – The best medicine for humans is LOVE. Someone asked – What if it doesn't work? He smiled and answered – Increase the dose."

When we're young, most of us don't give too much thought to our health, and then before we know it, and the older we become, it starts taking center stage. It seems everyone is talking about it; everyone is doing something about it. Whether joining some new cross-training fitness class, jumping onboard the juicing and cleansing craze, or following the diet du jour, everyone is trying some new prescription for better health.

As a teen I was concerned with my weight, as it seemed to fluctuate wildly on a daily basis. Most of my efforts into the realm of good eating and exercise were really just an attempt to lose 10 or 15 pounds so that I could fit into my jeans and not have to go up to the next dreaded size, or heaven forbid, grow out of the Junior sizes and get kicked up into those whole numbers, like 6, 8, and 10. Like most of the other teen girls I knew, I wanted to be liked, to be popular and to look good for the opposite sex. That meant being thin. Sometimes it meant doing really unhealthy things, like eating very little, taking diet pills and going on extremely restrictive diets. Ridiculous diets, like nothing but grapefruit, cabbage soup or carrots and celery for weeks. I have a feeling that a lot of you reading this can relate to me here, and are quietly shaking your heads, thinking, "Oh yeah, I tried that stupid one too!"

As the years rolled by and life became more demanding, good health meant more to me than just my physical size.

I soon came to realize the benefits of
stress reduction techniques such as
mediation and yoga to improve my mental
and emotional health. I practiced them
religiously for a time and the benefits were
undeniable. But these extremely beneficial
practices that I knew where doing me
a world of good, were somehow hard
for me to sustain. For whatever reason,
I would repeatedly sabotage myself and
slack off, once again waking up to my
old habit of coffee with cream instead of
crossed legs and meditation.

Then, because of the disappointment I
felt in myself due to my lack of willpower
or my sorry sense of self-worth, I was
embarrassed, lost faith in myself, and
sometimes just quit trying. It wasn't
until I began to study the ancient art of
Feng Shui, studied nutrition and bio-
individuality, and grasped the concept of
Wabi Sabi, that I understood that my life

was not about setting and meeting one goal after another. It was about living, loving, experimenting, learning, applying and sometimes, even discarding. And most importantly, I was told it was okay to take things little by little, to go with the natural rhythm and flow, and to slowly incorporate simple and mindful changes that would eventually reward me with sustainable improvements in my overall health. I felt a deeper sense of calm, hope and acceptance. Positivity seemed to fall into my lap and I quit beating myself up with the paddle of failure. When things weren't working, I merely accepted that perhaps I needed to try something different. I felt it was okay to be done with something and move on. Sometimes things just have an expiration date, plain and simple, and they are in no way a sign of failure or defeat.

Many years later, I started studying

nutrition to become a health coach. And
while I was taught over 90 dietary theories
and experimented with several eating
styles, such as veganism, vegetarianism,
macrobiotics, The Zone, and others, there
was something more that needed to be
addressed on this plate. My education
had taught me that there were two types
of food: primary food and secondary
food. Secondary food being the food we
actually consume through our mouths.
And yes, it is very important. But what we
were also taught is that our primary food,
things like healthy relationships, regular
physical activity, a fulfilling career and a
spiritual practice are just as important, and
sometimes even more so than the food
we eat to nourish our bodies. The way we
feed our hunger for play, touch, romance,
achievement, art, music, self-expression,
excitement, adventure, spirituality and love
are the things necessary to fill our soul and
satisfy our hunger for life, and all of these

combined, determine how enjoyable and healthy our lives can be.

The food we consume is only part of the health equation. We could be on the healthiest diet, eating all organic, serving up daily portions of broccoli and kale, and supplementing with chia seeds and super foods till the cows come home. But if we are in a loveless marriage or abusive relationship, hate our job, or are on the outs with friends or family, these things will begin to manifest in very unhealthy ways. From mundane headaches and depression to the most serious of conditions. Our physical, emotional and spiritual health is interconnected. When one suffers, they all suffer.

Most of us know intuitively what is good for us and what isn't. We know the benefits of a good diet, exercise, weight control, not smoking, and moderate alcohol consumption. No need to preach to the choir. But we do need to remind ourselves to listen to our bodies and make the best choices we can; for our body is indeed a temple, but we must first decide to treat it that way.

"The doctor of the future will be oneself."
— Albert Schweitzer

There are a zillion choices that we can make to help us achieve better health, and I could provide you an endless segment of that very long list. It would include things like:

- Getting a good night's sleep; which is so vital in the healing process.

- Drinking water; lots of it.

- Eating good food; real food, food that doesn't come out of a box or bag.

- Fresh air and exercise; moving in ways we truly enjoy.

- Breathing deep (air, being our main source of chi).

- Incorporating stress reducing activities in our lives.

- Smiling, and even better, laughing (which truly is the best medicine) as it not only feels absolutely fabulous, but actually breaks up emotional and energetic blockages in the body.

- Practicing gratitude and counting our blessings; and so much more.

So now, up to this point in my life, I have been taught the importance of feeding my body, mind and soul. From the way I feed my relationships, to the way I express myself creativity, how I give of myself, what I share with the world, where I find satisfaction and contentment with my place here on the planet. But I don't know if I truly acknowledged the importance of being loved, of loving others, and self-love when it comes to the impact it has on our health. I was reminded of this firsthand just recently.

When I was about 9 years old I met Virginia, who would become my very best friend, and to this day, she still is. We grew up together, shared secrets, knew everything there was to know about each other. Together, we went through first loves, first marriages, first divorces, the raising of our children, and the sharing of our families. Betty, Virginia's mother was a loving, wonderful woman who married her high school sweetheart at 17, had four children, never worked outside the home, and to her shock and dismay, was told by her husband when she was in her 50s, that he was leaving her. He told her that he never loved her and wanted out of the marriage. Needless to say, she was beyond devastated. He was all she had ever known;

he was the love of her life, and she had loved him every single day of it.

He left and Betty's life fell apart, and like Humpty Dumpty, she never was able to put it back together again. During the next 20 years she found comfort in her family and friends, but the love of a partner had left a deep void in her life. She never dated again. It was as if she fell victim to his last words, fatally wounded by his sharp tongue. Even though she had her family, she still went home alone each night, to sleep on her side of the queen size bed and would wake in the morning to a still, empty house.

A little over 3 months ago, suddenly, Betty was diagnosed with stage IV leukemia. Doctors told her she had maybe 6 weeks or so to live. Virginia went into denial mode, not believing this could happen to her mother, while it seemed Betty accepted her fate only a little too willingly. She wasn't going to fight it, that much was obvious.

Over the next few weeks, Betty was moved into Virginia's house. There they set up a wonderful living area for her, her own bedroom and bath, plus a reading/TV room for Betty to spend time watching her favorite old black and white movies or reading a good book. Virginia cooked for her, cared for her, took her out to lunch, out to shop, watched movies, they sat and held each other, cuddled together and laughed. Friends and family came by daily. Delicious meals were cooked and shared. The house was so full of love that it bounced off the walls.

I got a call from Virginia, "Please, you need to come up. She's leaving us. Hospice said she probably won't last the week." I cancelled a trip I had scheduled to fly up to Portland and instead got in my car and drove the 7 hours to her house. Betty was there, and looked relatively healthy. We sat around for a couple of days and talked, told stories, had meals together, and laughed. I even helped write up a Living Will for her, which she signed, and I witnessed. She seemed to be enjoying life. My few days there were coming to an end and I needed to leave the next morning. That night I gave Betty a hug, being careful not to squeeze her bruised and aching body too tight. I couldn't say goodbye. I didn't know how to say goodbye. It's one thing to say goodbye when you know that the future holds another hello. But this would be a final farewell, and I couldn't say anything, except "I love you." I held back my tears and only cried once we had helped her back to her room, making sure she was in her bed and we had closed the door. I drove off early the next morning, wondering if Betty would last the day.

Weeks followed and each day Hospice told Virginia that they were surprised Betty was still holding on, by all accounts and every lab report, she should be have been gone. They couldn't understand it. But the energy of the house was so soothing, dripping with love, honesty, and appreciation. The recognition that life was fragile and at this point, fleeting, was very apparent. While constant visitors streamed through the house, never leaving room for emptiness or despair, Betty went into a semi-coma. She died three days later. But she looked content. And beautiful. She must have been basking in this incredible love that had been lacking for so many years. I have to believe that if she would have had this kind of love in her life earlier she might not have fallen ill, she might have had a stronger will, and her health might not have been so at risk.

So maybe the Beatles were right, when they sang, "Love is all you need." I think I witnessed the miracle of love as I watched Betty stay alive, even though in those final weeks her doctors said she should not even have been here. It leaves me to wonder, if this amount of love had just been prescribed for her years earlier, might she still be here? It's been said that love is the most powerful medicine of all. So if this is true, then to ensure our good health, we should all be given a hefty dose of it daily.

Having and maintaining good health comes down to our physical, emotional and spiritual states being in balance. They say you can live without food for an indefinite period of time, maybe a month or so. More important is water, as you can only live without water for a matter of days, and the most vital of all is air, for without air we survive only minutes. But even if we have all of these elements, without love and our good health, it can seem like we're not really living. So, let's feed ourselves well, being open and receptive to love, and by sharing our love abundantly with others.

Revving Up Your Inner Engines
The Insider's Manual to a Healthier You

By Mary Jane Kasliner

"When health is absent, wisdom cannot reveal itself, art cannot manifest, strength cannot fight, wealth becomes useless, and intelligence cannot be applied."

—Herophilus

What if your body came with an owner's manual? What do you think it would include? Arguably, topics such as ideal weight, proper diet, exercise and sleep would be in the table of contents. Albeit important topics when it comes to health, something tells me that if we delve deeper we might find a section that moves beyond the physical. This section of the manual might look something like this:

- Look at your whole being rather than just your palpable being
- Acknowledge your thoughts and emotions

- Understand your purpose in life
- Create a relationship with Higher Power

Obviously this section sounds very different from the first perspective as the role of chieftain is higher self. When referencing this section of the manual it requires you to expand your focus beyond the physical and tune into the subtle energy body. This is the body that determines how healthy we really are.

Operating Systems

The Sacred Body

Vitruvian Man is perhaps Leonardo da Vinci's most famous work. It is the quintessential image of perfection. He explains his theories of Vitruvius, a first century architect who believed the proportions and measurements of the human body, which was divinely created, were perfect and correct. In this famous image, da Vinci draws a male figure whose outstretched limbs touch the circumference of a circle and the edges of a square. The navel falls within the exact center of the circle. This image is a reminder that human beings are perfect. These findings should not be surprising—after all, the head engineer, God, created the original designs. With that being said, our body is already wired for perfect health. It's simply up to us to maintain it.

The Head

It's All Gears, or Is It?

The first thing that comes to mind when referring to "the head" is the brain. The brain is associated with knowledge. Knowledge from a biblical perspective denotes understanding. To "know" something is to perceive or be aware of it. In scripture, knowledge carries the idea of deeper appreciation of something or someone. The knowledge of God is the most valuable knowledge a human being can possess. This belief is widely shared by many cultures and religions of the world.

The Toltecs, a Mesoamerican culture that dominated a state centered in Tula (what is today the southwest of the Mexican state Hildago) saw knowledge as a road to human development on every level. They believed a human being wasn't born to simply grow, reproduce and die, but rather to move towards a quest for knowledge and answer questions such as: *Who am I? Where do I come from? And where am I going?* Over time, the Toltec's polished the idea of the meaning of life through a complex system called *Tōltēcayōtl,* a set of knowledge aimed at achieving spiritual transcendence to a higher level. This was symbolically referred to as the four aspects of *Quetzalcoatl* cross representing the four life directions: the spiritual aspect with material aspect and the rational aspect with the intuitive.

The Toltecs were actually a group of scientists and artists who formed a society to explore spiritual knowledge. In *The Four Agreements*, Don Miguel Ruiz reveals four agreements based on Toltec philosophy that offer powerful modes to approach life in order to experience true freedom, health and happiness.

The first agreement, *Be Impeccable with Your Word*, is so profound. Let's face it, words are powerful. They can create and manifest things in your life, or they can cause self-limiting beliefs that lead to unnecessary suffering, ill health and unhappiness. Simply said, words are like seeds; once planted in your mind, they will grow and multiply. The question is—what's growing in your mind?

The Gospel of John says, *"In the beginning was the word, and the word was with God, and the word is God."* When you choose words that are falsehoods you go against yourself. Being impeccable with your words means you do not go against yourself. Repeated assaults against oneself lead to suffering, and suffering leads to illness.

The second agreement, *Don't Take Anything Personally*, can really test self-love. Whenever you take something personally, you believe whatever was said. Think about that for a moment. How many times have you suffered needlessly to the point of physical discomfort because you believed what was said about you? Understand that you chose to plant the seed. What others say is always about them and not you. There is always a choice to be made, and it comes back to how impeccable you are with your own words.

The third agreement, *Don't Make Assumptions*,

challenges what we assume to be true. Every time we make an assumption we believe it to be gospel. This unfolds as drama in our lives, followed by stress, suffering and ultimately physical and emotional discomfort. The easiest way to avoid making assumptions is to ask more questions.

The fourth agreement, *Always Do Your Best*, is the result of understanding and practicing the first three agreements. If you choose to do your best no matter what happens, then you will enjoy your life. When you do your best, you will love what you do. When you love what you are doing you are not looking for a reward or trying to impress others. This eliminates stress and ultimately you feel joyful, healthy and loving.

Upholding these four agreements requires discipline, commitment and steady maintenance. While these agreements seem simple to implement, in actuality they are very difficult to practice. However, it behooves us to take that leap of faith, as the rewards are immeasurable when it comes to feeling your best physically, mentally and spiritually.

The totality of being in alignment with these three aspects of self is the key to experiencing true health. When you start by aligning the spirit body, the physical body will follow. When the spirit is healthy it is the equivalent of fueling your car with high octane gasoline. The end result is a smoother ride and greater longevity.

Knowledge Maintenance

Indicator Lights

The authorized dealer or higher self has various warning lights that will trigger when knowledge maintenance is required. Based on day-to-day living habits, it is highly recommended to schedule your knowledge maintenance otherwise you may notice the following warning signals:

- Irritability
- Anxiety
- Fear
- Resentment
- Emotional and physical exhaustion

Each Day Stop for Maintenance:

- Find an area in your home where you will not be disturbed.

- Sit in an upright position on the floor with your legs crossed in front of you and your hands resting gently on your knees. If sitting on the floor is not an option then sit in a chair with both feet firmly planted on the ground.

- Allow your eyelids to gently close and begin to tune into your breath. Take three cleansing breaths: one for the spirit, one for the mind and one for the body.

- With the next several breaths, imagine a white ball of energy rising through your spine with the sound of "hum." Upon exhalation, visualize this white ball of energy descending your spine with the sound of "sa."

- Slowly turn your focus towards the midpoint of your forehead. Send your breath through this point and allow it to rise up through the crown of your head.

- Finish this meditation by visualizing the crown of your head opening like the thousand petals of a lotus flower. As the petals blossom, see the stream of universal knowledge flow into your head and descend into your body via your spine.

- Stay in this meditation for at

least 15 minutes. Add more time in meditation if indicator lights continue to flash.

The Heart

An Intricate Pump

The heart is an amazing organ that beats 108,000 times per day and pumps 1,900 gallons of blood through the body. It is the main cylinder that keeps the physical body alive. But our heart is more than a physical organ. It is part of the Etheric body – a subtle level of the physical body composed of various energies such as chi, prana, and subatomic particles known as quarks.

The heart is also part of the seven archetypical chakras, spinning wheels of lights that refer to one of our levels of consciousness. These original Indian chakras are symbolized by a specific lotus flower.

The heart chakra in Sanskrit is referred

to as *Anahata*. The literal interpretation is "unstricken" or not to hold anything or anyone too tight. This chakra point represents leaving the physical aspect and entering the mental. It is considered the true realm of human beings, the place where the spiritual meets the material world.

The subchakra point to the heart is called *Anandakanda* and symbolizes our ability to attract what our soul is longing for. Attracting what the soul longs for is the key behind loving what you do. This concept coincides with the aforementioned fourth agreement – *Always Do Your Best*.

The energy heart portrays unconditional love towards oneself and others; therefore, self-acceptance must occur before accepting others. Regardless of where we have been, or where we are going, we must accept ourselves in the present moment and acknowledge our value as members of the human family.

Heart Maintenance

Indicator Lights

The heart is the center of the body. It is the governing point between the physical and spiritual realm of existence. Opening up this point of the etheric energy body allows for total health to ensue. However, when this point is clogged it can literally and physically end life. Below are the indicators that this system is in need of maintenance:

- Jealousy
- Being overly protective
- Selfishness
- Conditional love
- Possessive feelings
- Anxiousness
- Misery
- Feelings of isolation
- High blood pressure
- Circulation issues

Stop for maintenance when these indicator lights begin to flash, otherwise you will be in for a downward spiral and repairs can be quite costly. Every heart is different so it is important that you be the judge of when you're in need of a tune-up.

Heart Tune-Up:

- Wear comfortable loose clothing.

- Sit in the middle of an open room (you will not want anything close enough to disrupt the energy body) and know that a subtle electromagnetic field surrounds your physical body.

- Quiet your mind by focusing on breathing through the heart. Let everything else go and allow your breath to invigorate your heart. Become one with the breath and one with the heart.

- Once you are completely one with
  the heart, begin to concentrate
  your breath in through your throat
  and the point between your eyes
  while still being aware of your
  heart. Become aware of where your
  breath originates – just above the
  belly in the solar plexus—and feel
  a widening of the breath through
  the entire length of your body from
  belly to throat.

- Now explore your breath further
  from the lower belly all the way up
  to the middle of your forehead. Feel
  the life and spirit in your body.

- Continue to move your breath
  further and encompass the
  expansion from the pelvic floor
  to the crown of the head all while
  being aware of the heart. Become
  one with your body.

- Now begin to breathe into the ground directly beneath you and extend that breath directly above you. Continue this breath as you connect to Mother Earth beneath you and Father Sky above you and become one with heaven and earth.

This meditation can be performed as frequently as you like. The key is to be aware when the indicators trigger in your life and cause pain and suffering.

Quick Heart Tune-Up

The Merriment Factor

When all else fails, go ahead and have a good laugh. Laughing releases endorphins in your brain, which chemically causes you to relax.

Think of laughter as an exercise routine for the heart and lungs. Not only does it stimulate the diaphragm by bringing more oxygen to the body, but it also releases a wave of mental stress recovery.

Having a healthy sense of humor goes a long way when it comes to your wellbeing. When you laugh, you will feel more relaxed and so will others. Most importantly, you can enjoy your own company.

Environment

Try creating a joyful environment at work and at home. This can be done with creative artwork that lends itself to conversation or paint colors that can literally make you happier. Splashes of bold colors such as orange or yellow stimulate joy and creativity. Add these as accent colors or go ahead and paint an entire room – and while you're at it, why not pipe in some music that puts a smile on your face and a twinkle in your eye.

Sensory Body

Perception Systems

The commonly recognized sensory systems are those for vision, hearing, somatic sensation (touch), taste and olfaction (smell). These are powerful systems that flow through the thalamus or "inner room" of the brain that regulates emotion and perception of discomfort or pleasure. There are some simple activation devices for the sensory system in your manual that can automatically improve your perception of an environment and elicit pleasant feelings.

Sensory Maintenance Devices

Nature's Secret

Time and time again, research reveals that environments can increase or reduce our stress, which in turn impacts our bodies. What you are seeing, hearing, smelling, tasting or touching at any moment cannot only impact your mood but how your nervous system, endocrine and immune systems are working.

The stress associated with an unpleasant environment can cause you to feel anxious, sad or even mad. This in turn can elevate blood pressure and create overall tension in the body. Warning! These are indicators lights that need immediate attention.

Daily Maintenance Devices:

Nature is one of the best devices to reverse the side effects of an unpleasant environment. Even viewing scenes of nature in artwork can reduce stress and induce feelings of pleasure. Here are simple devices to maintain your sensory systems:

- Spend time outdoors every day.

- Infuse the color green into your space. Looking at the color green can evoke the same relaxation as going for a stroll in the park.

- Choose landscape scenes in artwork or tapestries. These natural visuals connect us to each other and the larger world according to field studies conducted by Kuo and Coley at the Human-Environment Research Lab.

- Add fresh flowers, pine cones or sea shells to a vase. These natural elements uphold sacred geometric forms imbuing your environment with divine harmony.

- Incorporate a water fountain or fish tank into your living or working space. The sound quality evokes the feeling of a nearby stream.

- Diffuse pure essential flower oils into your environment. This is a powerful way to induce feelings of pleasure.

- Incorporate natural fabrics and furnishings in your interior design. It not only is healthier but it feels better to the touch.

- Choose local organic foods for your diet. These foods will not only taste better, but buying local and organic foods helps restore natural resources for a healthier planet and healthier YOU!

Humble Spark Plugs

Ignition to Running Your Body

In a car, these little buggers are so small and inconsequential looking, most people are happy to go along without giving their spark plugs a second thought – until they don't work. Suddenly, this tiny little part brings everything to a screeching halt. Well, not unlike the spark plugs for your car, our bodies have subtle energy wheels which act as spark plugs that fuel the physical and emotional body. If not serviced, they can bring your body to a screeching halt, too.

These wheels of light exist in our subtle etheric body, the non-material energetic counterpart to our physical body. In Sanskrit these energy centers or vortexes are known as chakras. There are many chakras, but seven main distinct centers are located along the main channel, or Sushumna, of our spine. These energy wheels are constantly working to absorb information from the surrounding environment. There are two lesser channels of energy – the Pingala on the right side of the body and the Ida on the left side – running parallel to the spinal cord. These wheels of energy both take up and collect prana (life force energy) and transform and pass it on to the physical body and organ systems.

Each chakra is associated with a certain part of the body, specific aspect of human behavior, and internal organ system. These energy wheels rotate at different frequencies relative to their location in the body and our awareness of how to integrate the characteristics associated with each chakra into our lives. The lower wheels are associated with fundamental emotions and needs, vibrating at a lower frequency. The higher wheels have a finer energy frequency as they correspond to higher mental and spiritual aspirations.

The openness and flow of energy through these wheels determines our state of health and empowers us on a physical, mental and spiritual level. Maintaining the efficiency of these energy centers is vital to keeping our bodies running smoothly.

Energy Wheel Maintenance Index:

Anything can throw this delicate energy system out of balance and when this happens there is a domino effect of physical and mental symptoms that can arise. Needless to say, this will take its toll on you and your wallet. Listed below is your energy wheel maintenance index and protocol maintenance routine.

- *Crown Chakra* is located at the top of the head and governs the brain, nervous system, right eye and pineal gland. It represents our higher consciousness and awareness of spirit. Warning lights will trigger when you are chronically fatigued or feel as though you lack purpose in life.

- *3rd Eye Chakra* is located between the eyebrows and also governs the brain, left eye, nose and ears. It represents our intuition, wisdom and self-knowledge. Warning lights will trigger with chronic headaches, seizures, learning disabilities, and being judgmental.

- *Throat Chakra* is located at the throat level and governs the thyroid, mouth, teeth, gums and shoulders. It represents our inner voice, responsibility and ability to communicate with others. Warning lights will trigger with chronic thyroid issues, hearing problems, stiff neck and constant difficulties with decision making.

- *Heart Chakra* is located in the cardiac plexus and governs the heart, circulatory system, breast, and diaphragm. It represents our ability to give, trust, be compassionate and love unconditionally. Warning lights will trigger with heart conditions, asthma, and upper back and shoulder pain.

- *Solar Plexus Chakra* is located just beneath the rib cage and above the stomach. It governs the small intestines, liver, gallbladder, kidneys, adrenals and stomach. It represents self-esteem, a sense of belonging, personal power and the ego. Warning lights will trigger with diabetes, arthritis, colon diseases, eating disorders, anxiety, fear of rejection and perfectionism.

- *Naval Chakra* is located at the base of the pubic bone. It governs the sexual organs, spleen, and pancreas. It represents our creative inspirations, pleasure, personal relationships and emotional identity. Warning lights will trigger with sciatic pain, pelvic pain, urinary problems, menstrual issues, shyness, feelings of guilt or blame and sexual obsessions.

- *Root Chakra* is located at the base of the spine between genitals and anus.

It governs the legs, bones, prostate, kidney and adrenals. It represents our instincts, basic survival mechanisms and our ambitions in life. Warning lights will trigger when feeling ungrounded, fearful, being obsessed with comfort, insomnia, depression and immune diseases.

Maintenance Routine:

Follow this maintenance routine twice a week to keep your humble energy wheel systems in tip-top shape:

- Find a quiet place where you will not be disturbed.

- Either sit in a relaxed crossed-legged position on the floor (meditation position) or lie down on your back with legs extended and arms resting along the sides of your body with palms facing upwards.

- Allow your eyelids to gently close
  and tune in to your breathing. Let
  the breath originate from your
  stomach and rise up into your lungs.

- Once you feel totally relaxed,
  send your focus to the root
  chakra point at the base of your
  spine and visualize a red ball of
  energy spinning in this area. Feel
  a sensation of being firmly rooted
  into the earth. Repeat the sound
  vibration of "lum" several times.
  Then leave that ball of red light and
  move upwards to the naval point.

- At the naval point begin to visualize
  an orange ball of energy encircling
  the naval area. Allow this ball of
  energy to spin here for a few minutes
  and clear out any negative feelings
  you may have about yourself or
  the opposite sex. Chant the mantra

"vum" either aloud or silently and then move your focus to the solar plexus region.

- At the solar plexus visualize a pure yellow light of energy such as the sun washing through the solar plexus. Sense how powerful you are. Allow your inner warrior to rise. Chant the sound mantra "rum" for a few breaths and then turn your focus upwards to the heart center.

- At the heart center visualize the color emerald green. Allow it to imbue the entire chest cavity and feel love spreading out from your heart to surround your entire being. Chant the mantra "yum" and then allow your focus to rise into your throat.

- At the throat point, visualize a pure sky blue color and let it saturate the entire region of your neck. As this ball of blue energy spins here, imagine that you express yourself with ease and allow your voice to be heard. Take a few moments here and chant the sound "hum" before moving your focus to the point between your brows.

- At the 3rd eye point (between the brows), imagine a vortex of indigo color moving deep into the mid-brain while tapping into your intuition. Take a moment here and chant the mantra "kshum" before moving your focus to the crown of your head.

- Once at the crown of your head, imagine the petals of a beautiful lotus flower opening one by one, blooming with a vibrant white light connecting you to a higher source –

to God – and chant the sound "om."

- You can end this meditation by drawing a white light of energy in through the crown of your head and allow it to move through the entire body as you tap into the feelings of gratitude.

So there you have it! Refer to this as an owner's manual for healthy spiritual and energetic systems in order to keep your physical body in good working order for your entire lifetime, and beyond. After all, God designed the human body as a finely tuned instrument resilient to many things on this earth, but he designed the spirit body to last forever.

The Wisdom Buffet Writers Biographies

Previous Books by Authors:

*Happiness Chronicles -
Short Stories and Recipes for a Happy Life*

Janet Mitsui Brown

Janet is a life-long artist. She is an author/
illustrator of a children's book entitled
Thanksgiving at Obaachan's, a columnist
in two Southern California online news
journals, Culver City Crossroads &
California Crusader News, and a published
writer in the Los Angeles Times, the Los
Angeles based Rafu Shimpo newspaper,
and other journals.

Janet is also the co-owner of Tani B
Productions, Inc., a film/publishing
production company, and its subsidiary
The Joy of Feng Shui, where she is the
principal practitioner, advising individuals
and businesses on how to enhance their
lives utilizing Feng Shui principles.

Janet is a tai chi international gold medalist,
and continues to study with the Wushu
Center in Los Angeles and Hanzhou, China.
Janet formally studies Feng Shui with Helen

& James Jay at Feng Shui Designs, Master Larry Sang of the American Feng Shui Institute, and His Holiness Grandmaster Lin Yun and Her Holiness Khadro Crystal Chu Rinpoche and their disciples, with the Yun Lin Temple.

Based on her experiences, Janet offers consultations in tai chi gong, feng shui, and meditation. Her writings on these subjects can be viewed on her website, and in her ongoing news columns. Janet works with her husband, actor Roger A. Brown, and her daughter Tani, a writer, formerly with Google, and presently a Fulbright Scholar in Southeast Asia.

Katherine Graham

Katherine Graham is a Lifestyle Enhancer
and Modern Feng Shui Practitioner
based in Atlanta, Georgia. Katherine is
known for her powerful, practical and
personalized approach to Classical Feng
Shui. She is currently writing her first
book on Feng Shui, due out in 2015.
Connect with Katherine on Facebook
and Twitter under Haven Feng Shui,
which is also the name of her private
Feng Shui consulting company. And, if
you're interested in reading about Classical
Feng Shui with a Western twist, check out
her blog titled, Feng Shui for the Type
A where Katherine shares her Feng Shui
tips and expounds on her motto: "Dismiss
Dogma, Seek Results."

Mary Jane Kasliner

Mary Jane Kasliner graduated from
Skidmore College with a degree in Health
Science and Union College with a degree
in Applied Sciences. After nearly 20 years
of being a health care practitioner, Mary
Jane decided to shift her focus to the
disciplines of feng shui and yoga.

She studied Western Feng Shui at the De
Amicis School in Philadelphia and Classical
Feng Shui at both the New York School
of Feng Shui and Feng Shui Institute of
London. In 2008 Mary Jane finished her
200 hour national teacher training program
in Hatha Yoga at the Center of Health
and Healing and Personal Revolution
Baron Baptiste program at Yoga Bliss.
Several years afterwards, she completed
her Mastery of Meditation teacher training
program under Master Anmol Mehta.

In 2005 she opened Body Space Alignment,

a feng shui and yoga consulting company. Her clients include some of Manhattan's elite. She later established the Teaching Tortoise School of Feng Shui that offers certifications in Classical Feng Shui.

In 2009, Mary Jane was part of Seane Corn's Off the Mat and Into The World Humanitarian effort to Uganda. Mary Jane raised thousands of dollars for orphaned children due to war and AIDS in Uganda.

Mary Jane has received world-wide media coverage from the Associated Press for her work. She has been interviewed on TV and radio many times and is the author of 3 books, 15 Feng Shui training CD's, and a Feng Shui design CD.

Located in Ocean, New Jersey, Mary Jane loves to play golf and travel whenever she can. Mary Jane can be contacted at www.fengshuiyoganj.com.

Kim Klein

Kim's background is in the healing arts, with areas of study ranging from Massage Therapy to Chinese Medicine. Later, as a student of the Rhodec International School of Interior Design, she became acutely aware of the difference in an environment that looks good ascetically as opposed to an environment that actually nourishes our well-being. She started reading every book she could find on the subject of Feng Shui and then attended and graduated from the three year BTB (Black Tantric Buddhist) Masters Training Program, studying the teachings of Professor Lin Yun under teachers Steven Post, Barry Gordon and Edgar Sung. She has also attended many advanced Feng Shui workshops by various teachers, including Seann Xenja, Richard Feather Anderson, Roger Green and others.

Kim is an award-winning author and has written ongoing Feng Shui columns for several newspapers, including the Napa Valley Register and the Santa Barbara NewsPress. She has authored a variety of very popular blogs, including The Coffee Shop Diary along with co-publishing her first novel and screenplay, Nine Degrees North, in March of 2013. Kim recently finished her second screenplay, Twenty-One Sunsets. Her passion for writing is complemented by her experience in a variety of fields, such as Feng Shui, Chinese medicine, multi-media art and design. She is currently working on a novel, Letters From York and has a book in the works about Feng Shui combined with other modalities, entitled Life by Design - creating and living the life you desire.

Located in Santa Barbara, California, Kim currently practices as a Certified Feng Shui Consultant, working with both residential and corporate environments. She is also a Certified Health Coach and has clients ranging from the Napa Valley to Miami. (Kim Klein, www. kimkleinfengshui.com, or on Facebook at, Kim Klein Fusion Feng Shui.

Belinda Mendoza

Belinda Mendoza is a certified Feng Shui consultant trained in the US and China in East and West Schools of Feng Shui with Professor Lin Yin, Jon Sandifer and Raymond Lo. She is also a Reiki Master and applies energy work to all her consultations.

Belinda is a graduate of the University of Texas at Austin and a former social worker and corporate sales leader. She left those professions and began her Feng Shui business in 2000. She is a problem solver and has been helping businesses and people create positive change in their lives through feng shui analysis, redesigns, staging and space clearing for over 17 yrs.

Her passion is her yorkies and she runs a monthly dog group for 7 years helping owners socialize their pets. Belinda has a new book published through Hay House called, *"Feng Shui For The Loss of a Pet, Restoring Balance during Grief and Loss, A Personal Journey".*

Belinda is also a Big Sister in the BBS program for 9 yrs. now. She can be reached at www.designforenergy.com or belinda@ designforenergy.com.

Belinda resides in Austin, Texas and always offers a free 30 minute phone consultation for anyone interested in Feng Shui or her services. 512-740-1251. She wishes you Fortunate Blessings!

Mia Staysko

Mia is a professional Feng Shui consultant, artist and designer. Through her company, White Lotus Interiors, she helps people to create spaces that support their bodies, and their souls. Mia's goal is to help people to transform their lives and their spaces through conscious design.

Mia is certified in BTB Feng Shui, studying with His Holiness Grandmaster Lin Yun, Katherine Metz, James Jay and David Kennedy. She has additionally studied traditional Chinese methods, Flying Stars Feng Shui, 4 Pillars Astrology, 9 Star Ki and BaZi with Jon Sandifer and Dr. David Lai. Mia has a keen interest in yoga, numerology and all things spirit-lifting.

Mia is the founding Director of the Sacred Lotus School of Feng Shui and an active member of the International Feng Shui Guild.

Mia blogs on design, Feng Shui and other uplifting topics at www.livingfengshui.ca and produces the digital Living Feng Shui Magazine.

James (Jim) Thomas, MBA

Jim has become a successful small business entrepreneur who continues to build and grow businesses. His specialty is computer science however, he went back to school to receive a masters degree in business administration, then became a feng shui consultant.

Jim and Katie own www. fengshuiemporium.com, www.luckycat. com, and www.fengshuidirectory.com. Jim also saw a great opportunity with Amazon/ Kindle Publishing and contacted other feng shui authors for help writing this series of books. The collaboration of authors are known as The Wisdom Buffet Writers.

Jim enjoys spending time at his home in Missouri, family, friends as well as his customers from around the world. He loves hiking, water sports, traveling, and exercising.

A special thanks goes to his wife, Katie

and his kids, the love of his life. Jim's business coach, Shawn Chhabra, who has guided and helped his business knowledge and to his family and friends for their unwavering love and support.

Angi Ma Wong

The daughter of a diplomat who grew up in New Zealand, Taiwan, NY/NJ, Washington, D.C., finally settling in Los Angeles, her namesake city. Angi started five businesses in 1989, including being a publisher/author and an intercultural and Feng Shui consultant to over 200 real estate developers globally, hundreds of individuals, diverse business and industry clients.

She is the award-winning and best-selling author of 28 titles, including 15 on Feng Shui such as her best-selling Feng Shui Dos and Taboos series, as well as inspirational, children's, historical and business books. Her Survivor's Secrets to Health & Happiness is a four-book award-winner.

Known as the Feng Shui Lady (R), Angi has appeared on OPRAH, Regis, Redbook, PEOPLE, TIME and over 600 print,

broadcast and internet features, and is one
of the few Asian Americans on the global
speaking circuit on a variety of topics.

Visit Us

www.TheWisdomBuffet.com

www.ingramcontent.com/pod-product-compliance
Lightning Source LLC
LaVergne TN
LVHW051734080426
835511LV00018B/3061